Ironman Made Easy

Ironman Edition

Ironman Made Easy

by Paul Van Den Bosch

Published by Meyer & Meyer Sports

Ironman and M-dot are registered trademarks
of World Triathlon Corporation

British Library Cataloguing in Publication Data
A catalogue record for this book is available from the British Library

Paul Van Den Bosch
Ironman Made Easy
Oxford: Meyer & Meyer Sport (UK) Ltd., 2007
ISBN 10: 1-84126-111-4
ISBN 13: 978-1-84126-111-9

© 2007 by Meyer & Meyer Sport (UK) Ltd.
Aachen, Adelaide, Auckland, Budapest, Graz, Johannesburg,
New York, Olten (CH), Oxford, Singapore, Toronto
Member of the World
Sports Publishers' Association (WSPA)
www.w-s-p-a.org
Printed and bound by: B.O.S.S Druck und Medien GmbH, Germany
ISBN 10: 1-84126-111-4
ISBN 13: 978-1-84126-111-9
E-Mail: verlag@m-m-sports.com
www.m-m-sports.com

Contents

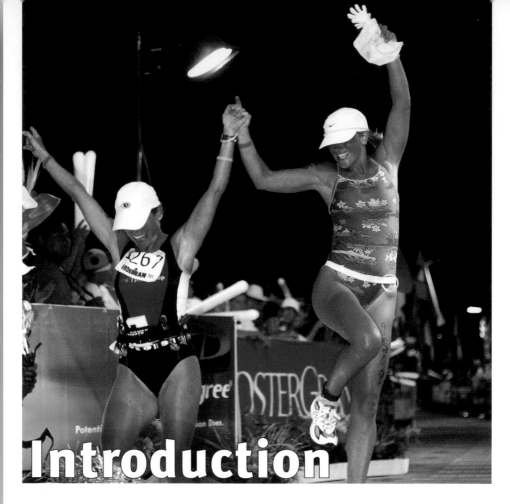

Introduction

Extreme physical performances have always appealed to the imagination of a lot of people. Even today many people take up jogging to chase the ultimate dream of being able to finish a marathon one day. The 42,195 kilometer race has enjoyed a mythical, almost heroic and unattainable status for a long time.

This is in large part due to the story that supposedly created this exhausting run. According to the Greek historian Herodotus, in the year 490 BC a Greek soldier ran from Marathon to Athens to communicate the victory of the Greek army over the Persian. Upon arrival, he was only able to say "we have overcome," whereupon he dropped dead.

Almost 2500 years later, a fairly similar incident occurred. Julie Moss totally collapsed in 1982 during the Hawaii Ironman, only a few meters before the finish after trying to complete the last hectometers, stumbling and crawling. Fortunately, this story ended less dramatically, but a new great myth was born. Hundreds of fanatics, later followed by thousands of others, threw themselves at this ultimate endurance test. The 10-hour finish time was rapidly reduced to 9 hours, and a few of the greatest champions even completed the whole track in less than 8 hours.

The always-improving performance level was, of course, only possible thanks to an equally increasing training load. Weekly totals of more than twenty hours of training are the rule rather than the exception for a lot of triathletes.

The question, however, is whether this huge investment of time is really necessary to complete the Ironman distance. Should crossing the finish of such a tough race remain an unfulfilled dream for those athletes who, due to a busy professional life, have considerably less training time at their disposal?

This book will show that the completion of an Ironman is not only feasible for professional and semi-professional athletes, but for every athlete committed to the task. Obviously, a certain time investment will always remain necessary to accomplish this almost 226-kilometer exhausting battle in a responsible manner.

But with good time management, even busy sport-loving people must be able to spend the time needed to prepare for this race. I claim that a program of eight training sessions per week, with maximum weeks of between eight to fourteen hours of training will be sufficient.

Being a coach I think it is very important that my athletes understand what they are doing in training at every moment, and that they particularly have a decent insight into the reason for every training session. This demands a basic knowledge of the complete training program.

In a way, every reader of this book is an athlete of mine. Therefore, I have tried to every subject needed to succeed in your ultimate challenge in an understandable way.

Because it will especially boil down to you using your time as efficiently as possible, you will first get ten important tips concerning your time management.

Answers will also be provided to a lot of obvious and less obvious questions.

First, how can you train as efficiently and purposefully as possible for three different disciplines? Which training sessions will give you the highest output in the shortest possible time.

> How do I best divide the different training sessions into a week? Which material do I need to start preparing for an Ironman?
>
> Why are slow training sessions preferred to more intensive training sessions?
>
> How do I determine my optimum training intensity? Do I have to use a heart rate monitor for this?

Particular attention is given to the importance of correct nutrition and fluid intake, not only during the race, but also during and after the training sessions.

Naturally, overtraining is also extensively discussed. Nevertheless, the preparation for this race distance will demand a lot of yourself, especially if we consider the combination professional life/training. The risk of overtraining and overloading injuries will thus never be far away.

Although the attentive reader will be able to compose a training program on his own using all this information, I have nevertheless added a chapter with detailed training programs.

These diagrams are set up in such a way that, with a minimum but necessary time investment, a maximum output can be gained: finishing an Ironman. Let these training programs be a guideline to realize your ultimate challenge.

Good luck!

Paul Van Den Bosch

CHAPTER 1

Time Management

To reach the finish of an Ironman distance race is obviously no piece of cake. To be an Ironman finisher, you will have to spend a considerable number of hours every week to physically prepare for the challenge.

You'll have to find a balance between your work, your private life (family) and your training. At times you will wonder how to plan all the necessary training sessions needed while trying to keep your priorities straight about all the other aspects of your life.

It should thus be clear that an extensive time management plan is the key to realizing your Ironman goals, especially if you have a busy professional life. But the preparation for such a heavy endurance test does not have to have a negative effect on your professional and your private life. The time you spend training will not be lost, but rather will have the following positive results:

1. If your training program is properly set up for you, you will definitely get fitter and more vigorous. You will soon realize a higher output in a shorter time in your job, and you will feel better in your private life.

2. Successful training for such a prestigious goal increases your confidence, your self-esteem and your mental strength. As a result, you will work more efficiently and be more in charge of your life.

3. Preparing for an Ironman distance event will incite you to a healthier lifestyle, and your improved fitness will allow you to work at a faster rhythm and find more time in your day.

10 tips for good time management

1. Set your priorities

Good time management starts with setting priorities. Before you start the preparation for an Ironman distance, you need to examine how important this aim is to you. You should not only be convinced that you want to reach the finish, but also that you need to invest sufficient time to realize this aim.

Therefore you should have a critical look at your work situation and your private life. Try to decide if you are willing to disregard other matters in favor of the training sessions, and if these training sessions can be scheduled realistically in your calendar. If the answer to these questions is yes, then go for it!

2. Clarify your goal

Communicate your aim to prepare for an Ironman distance to your colleagues, and clarify the personal importance of this goal to your family as well. The understanding of these both parties will enable you to find time for your training in a more relaxed way, and your output will increase in all areas.

3. Make a clear distinction between working hours and your time

If you prepare thoroughly for an Ironman distance, you must realize that it is not possible if training only in between (and during) working hours. You will need to utilize most of your spare time outside your job to realize this objective. The output of your training can only be maximized if you are both physically and mentally committed to your training.

This does not mean you have to banish thoughts of work during long, easy training sessions. This is actually a time when new and productive ideas often arise.

4. Plan your training sessions before/after your working hours if possible

It does not make much sense to plan training sessions during lunch breaks. This leads to restricted, rapid training sessions under high time pressure, which can cause significant additional stress. Stress slows down recovery capacity dramatically. Moreover, if you have too little time to eat, the essential intake of calories, sugars and fluids will be incomplete.

It"s better to plan training on weekdays before or after work. Training during the morning hours ispreferred. You'll be able to start your job energetically if you have already completed an easy 45 minute run or some serious swim training in the mornings.

Training sessions afterwork are only profitable if you can start early in the evening. If you train too late at night, you will disturb your normal family life, and risk not sleeping well. A healthy night's rest is absolutely essential to processing all your training labor.

5. Use your time at work efficiently

Stick to the traditional guidelines of time management at work, such as:

1 set priorities, and spend the most time on the highest priorities

2 limit unproductive telephone conversations

3 learn to say 'no'

4 limit social talk

5 organize your e-mail traffic in a structured manner

Although this is difficult for some people, now may be the time to delegate more tasks to others. That way you may be able to start your work day a little bit later, or finish somewhat earlier.

6. Plan in advance all your training sessions for the last six months before the race

You could never prepare yourself successfully for an Ironman distance race if you tried to plan your training sessions week to week, or day to day. Before you realize it, your calendar will be full, with no more time left to train.

You can only assure regularity in your training sessions if you plan your training hours weeks or even months in advance, clearly indicated in your calendar!

Most of the time it's best to stick to a certain number of fixed hours per week for swimming, for example. You'll have to complete at least two swim training sessions a week, of which one should be on the weekend. Mark these hours in advance on your calendar, and consider them holy.

Mark your training hours during the weekend as well, so you have a clear picture of the time you can spend with your family and on your training. If you have planned a long slow distance training session on Sunday, possibly with a number of running mates, consistently keep this training session on your calendar.

7. Impose on yourself a serious self-discipline
Self-discipline is essential. Undoubtedly you will sometimes be inclined to postpone the training sessions, and to plan another activity during the fixed training hours. Only fatigue and illness should be reasons to deviate from your fixed training plan.

8. Plan your difficult meetings and appointments during your recovery day
As soon as the overall weekly training has reached a certain level, it is absolutely necessary to plan a fixed recovery day. Since your heaviest training sessions will occur during the weekend, Monday is the most suitable recovery day. Use this day to plan tasks, such as appointments which can lead to overtime or which must be done in the evening.

9. Plan the largest part of your training sessions during the weekend
The weekend is perfectly appropriate to plan the long slow distance sessions (cycling and running), and to complete two training sessions a day. You should be able to do more than 50% of your total training volume during the weekend.

10. Plan a number of days off during the toughest training weeks

This not only provides the possibility to train harder, but also improves your recovery from these tough training sessions.

CHAPTER 2

Various Types of Training

Participating in an Ironman distance event is no easy task. Every person who trains for the Ironman distance eventually has to put in a certain training quantity. There are no shortcuts. However, given your rather restrictive time to train, every minute should generate optimal output. Efficient training is the answer! In other words, your training set up must include the correct training forms in the correct proportions.

Energy supply of the body

To get a better idea of the different training forms available for triathletes, you need to have the correct insight into the energy supply of the body.

We can consider the body as a constantly working engine. To keep this engine going you always need to have enough fuel. Our bodies need several types of fuel, depending on the duration and the intensity of the effort.

Energy for the short and intense efforts

A limited quantity of energy can bestacked up in our body in the form of ATP (adenosinetriphosphate) and CP (creatin phosphate). This energy is immediately available, but after a few seconds of exercise, is already consumed. If the effort lasts longer than a few seconds, another energy supply must be utilized, namely glycogen.

Glycogen consists of carbohydrates piled up in the muscles and the liver. If the effort is intense and prolonged, then lactic acid is formed in the muscles. The accumulation of lactic acid presents you with a feeling that your muscles are blocking, and forces you to either stop the effort or at least dramatically scale back the intensity.

This feeling is very intense when you climb a short, steep slope at full speed, for example. After one to two minutes, not only do your legs hurt, but your arms start feeling extremely heavy. The muscles are completely full of lactic acid and it becomes impossible, in spite of all will power, to continue cycling at the same pace.

The oxidation of the above mentioned energy sources takes place without the mediation of oxygen. Therefore this is called your **anaerobic energy supply**.

Energy for long-term efforts to low intensity

When the effort lasts longer, and therefore the intensity is lower, the body continues to appeal to multiple sources of energy. On the one hand, your body continues to draw partially on the oxidation of carbohydrates, but on the other hand, and this is interesting for triathletes, it also draws to a great extent on the oxidation of fatty acids.

The big difference between the energy supply for short-term efforts with high intensity is 1) that the amount of energy now available is much larger, and therefore much more slowly consumed, and 2) that this kind of energy is provided with the mediation of oxygen. We call this your aerobic energy supply.

The two largest energy sources are, therefore, fatty acids and carbohydrates. Which of these two energy sources will be utilized by the body depends initially on the intensity of the effort.

For a long-term effort of low intensity, energy will mainly be provided by oxidation of fatty acids. When the intensity of the effort rises, the share of carbohydrate oxidation will increase. If the carbohydrate supply is sufficient, it can provide energy for approximately 90 minutes. Its stock is therefore relatively limited. After a while the body must switch to oxidation of fatty acids.

The feeling that accompanies this change of energy supply by carbohydrates to energy supply by fatty acids is known as the infamous "punch of the hammer" or as "hitting the wall".

This is caused by the fact that for the same quantity of oxygen taken in, fatty acids release less energy than carbohydrates. The moment your carbohydrates are consumed, you suddenly obtain less energy without warning. This feels like having extremely heavy legs.

The fat store in the body is seemingly inexhaustible. When a triathlete is better trained for long distances, he will still be able to utilize this fat supply for a higher effort because the oxidation is more efficient than for untrained athletes.

In other words, a trained triathlete can save his carbohydrate supply longer, whereas a beginner starts consuming his carbohydrates much sooner.

Good aerobic endurance mainly serves efforts of relatively low intensity and long duration. "Relatively" indicates that the triathlete's degree of training must be taken into account. Low intensity for a well-trained triathlete could mean high intensity for a beginner.

Conclusion:

The energy source utilized by our body during physical efforts depends on:

- The intensity of the effort
- The duration of the effort
- The situation stipulated by nutrition (extra glycogen in the body)
- The degree of training

Various types of training

Below the different types of training will be discussed. Those training types that appeal to aerobic endurance, and which are done at rather low intensity, will be taken into particular consideration in your training program. Training sessions at a high intensity will inevitably lead to overload injuries.

Only athletes who have the ability to handle a significantly higher training volume, and have a very broad training foundation, can fit in the more intensive training types in their training set-up.

Recovery training

Recovery training is carried out in order to recover from preceding training sessions. The intensity is very low, and the training volume limited. These training sessions help remove waste products in the muscles and are generally preferred to passive recovery.

The importance of the recovery training cannot be underestimated. You should train hard in order to obtain results, but the eventual training impact can be only realized during the (active) recovery period.

A real recovery training session never lasts longer than 60 to 90 minutes on the bike, 20 to 40 minutes running and swimming. It depends on your degree of training. But if you cycle more than 90 minutes, for example, you cannot consider this recovery training, even for well-trained people. This should be looked upon as endurance training.

Particularly after intense run training sessions, doing recovery training on the bicycle or in the swimming pool is ideal. The movement on the bike and while swimming does not put additional strain on the muscles.

Aerobic endurance training

The perfect means to improve aerobic endurance capacity is aerobic endurance training. As mentioned before, this kind of endurance is the basic physical characteristic a triathlete should develop because it mobilizes the fat supply. Aerobic endurance training also forms the basis for all other more intensive training sessions.

Aerobic endurance capacity is often indicated by the maximal oxygen uptake (VO_2max). This parameter indicates how much oxygen can be incorporated in the muscle fibers (mainly the active muscles) of the triathlete at maximum effort. VO_2max, considered absolutely, is expressed in liters per minute. Because a very muscular triathlete can take in more oxygen (considered absolutely) than a light triathlete with less muscle mass, VO_2max is divided by the weight and is expressed in ml./min/kilogram. This is the relative capacity of oxygen uptake.

High VO$_2$max indicates a large capacity to oxidize energy supplies (carbohydrates and fatty acids). This is of course favorable to making long-term efforts. Measuring the maximum capacity of oxygen intake is rather time-consuming and provides no absolute value judgment concerning the aerobic capacity of the cyclist. However, it is common belief that VO$_2$max of 6oml/min.kg is a base requirement to achieve good results as a triathlete.

Aerobic endurance training can be subdivided into three levels:
Aerobic Endurance Training level 1 (AET1), Aerobic Endurance Training level 2 (AET2) and Aerobic Endurance Training level 3 (AET3)

- **AET1,** also known as Long Slow Distance (LSD), is very important for a triathlete. These are training sessions which last a very long time, generally longer than a race. The pace is relatively low, so you can easily chat during training. Energy is mainly provided by oxidation of fatty acids.

- In **AET2** as well, the training pace remains relatively low, but somewhat higher than in the LSD. Although oxidation of fatty acids is still essential for energy supply, the share of oxidation of carbohydrates increases. Through this type of training the triathlete prepares himself for the more intensive training ahead.

The AET1 and AET2 levels are very important because they will allow the triathlete to swim, cycle and run at a higher pace on the basis of fat metabolism, meaning swimming, cycling and running without the carbohydrate store being utilized.

These training forms are, of course, important for racing the Olympic distance. These races last about two hours, and often much longer.

But these training forms count even more in the preparation for Ironman distance races. In this case it is essential to swim, to run and to cycle at the highest possible intensity without addressing too much of the carbohydrate supply.

When preparing for the Ironman distance, training sessions on the bike, for example, can last as much as five to seven hours!

• **AET3** sessions are shorter than the AET1 and AET2 sessions, and the intensity is significantly higher. The triathlete has a less comfortable feeling, breathing rhythm is quicker and talking becomes more difficult.

This training takes place in the area under the threshold (see below), and has a positive influence on carbohydrate metabolism. These high intensity endurance training sessions move the endurance limit, i.e. you can swim, run and cycle at a higher speed for a longer time without lactic acid piling up.

An AET3 session on the bike, not including warm-up and cool-down time, generally lasts 60 to maximum 120 minutes, while running and

swimming lasts 20 to 40 minutes. This prepares the triathlete for both Olympic distance and the Ironman distance.

As the race season approaches, the AET3 sessions will gain importance. Their share should never account for more than 10 to 20 percent of the total training volume.

Fartlek

Fartlek or "speed play" is a form of interval training. Interval training is a training principle in which strain and recovery are systematically varied. In a speed play this alternation takes place instinctively. You will, for example, take into account the nature of the track, and build in rhythm changes during your training.

Whether training for aerobic or anaerobic endurance depends on the intensity of the high intensity segments.

HINT:
Fartlek is a playful and pleasant way to train for endurance. For a triathlete, training for aerobic endurance is quintessential. Therefore you must make sure that the intensity of this training session is not too high.

Tempo endurance training (bike)

Tempo endurance training (or threshold training) sessions are sessions carried out at the threshold, using repetitions of approximately 5 to 15 minutes. These are intensive training sessions which have a particularly favorable influence on the oxidation of carbohydrates as an energy source in the body.

You should distinguish threshold training on a flat track from threshold training uphill. On a flat track the intensity of these training sessions is just below and right on the threshold. On a hilly track, the training heart rate can be somewhat higher (therefore above the threshold) because when cycling uphill more muscle groups cooperate actively to make the effort.

Example of threshold training for a triathlete preparing for an Ironman distance:

- 30 min AET1 – 15 min AET2
- 4 to 6 times 15 min to high tempo, recovery 5 min easy riding. Make sure that the tempo is such that you can still ride during the last 10 minutesas rapidly as during the first 10 min!
- 30 min cooling down

This type of training sessions you only do during the last phase of the training set-up, approximately 6 to 4 weeks before the race. Earlier on you obviously stick to AET1, AET2 and AET3 training sessions.

Tempo interval training (run)

Doing the tempo interval run means you run a part of the distance of the upcoming race at a tempo equal to or faster than the race tempo. These distances are repeated, with a short recovery period in between which only allows incomplete recovery.

If you are, for example, capable of running 10 kilometers in 40 minutes (4 minutes a kilometer), then you will run 8 times 1000 meters at a speed of 3:55- 4 minutes. Between the repetitions you run 200 to 400 meters very relaxed.

Remark:

Such training sessions are very straining for the body, which is why they are not suitable for triathletes who only have limited training time at their disposal.

Only athletes who train very often could dare trying this type of training. These are especially useful for those athletes who are preparing for an Olympic distance race.

Submaximal (or extensive) interval training (cycling)

In submaximal (or extensive) interval training, the training load is systematically varied with (active) recuperation. The intensity of the training is above the threshold, but remains submaximal. The duration of the strain is between 30 seconds and 5 minutes, the number of repetitions is rather high and the recovery period between the efforts is short.

These training sessions are more important for the Olympic distance than for the Ironman distance

High intensity (or intensive) interval training

High intensity interval training is the perfect way to improve **anaerobic endurance capacity**. High intensity interval training actually teaches the body to cope with this lactic acid so that its piling-up is better endured. The anaerobic endurance capacity is therefore very important for efforts of high intensity and short duration.

This base characteristic is best trained by doing successive short-term efforts (30 sec to 90 sec) at very high, even maximum intensity. The number of repetitions is low (3 to 5 times) and the pause between the successive efforts is incomplete, so that the lactic acid has not been removed entirely when the next effort is started.

Triathletes who prepare for the Ironman distance have no profit training this form of endurance, especially because these training sessions, if carried out too often, have a negative impact on the aerobic endurance capacity.

Note: The Threshold

The term "threshold" causes quite a lot of confusion. The term threshold implies a heart rate which borders both the aerobic and the anaerobic energy supply level. Threshold training means training in the aerobic-anaerobic area. These training sessions are very effective to extend stamina, i.e. being able to perform without "going into the red".

CHAPTER 3

Training Program

You can subdivide your training set-up for the Ironman distance into two large phases:
* the general preparation period
* the specific preparation period

The general preparation period

Your goal is to finish an Ironman distance. To complete this task successfully within one year you must, at the start of your specific preparation, make sure you have a sound base for each of the three disciplines. This means that you must at least be able (separately) to run for 60 minutes without stopping, to cycle continuously for 180 minutes and to swim 2000 meters without any breaks. This last discipline in particular is difficult for a lot of novice triathletes. That is why, before you start the real preparation, you may need to attend an in-depth technical course in swimming.

The specific preparation period

The specific preparation period starts approximately 6 months (24 weeks) before the race.

First, a thorough medical check-up is essential. You must be certain that your blood values are at appropriate levels.

If you are determined to be healthy and fit, you are ready for some hard work. Your goal should be to fully develope your aerobic endurance. Therefore it is particularly important not to train too intensively, and instead put the emphasis on the training types AET1, AET2 and AET3.

Especially at the beginning of this specific preparation period, bike training does not yet really get much consideration. This is partly because for many triathletes the weather conditions in the winter and spring often don't allow long bike training sessions. It is also possible to build up your cycling condition in a shorter time period than your swimming and running. Therefore, it's best to first take into account these latter disciplines.

Nevertheless bike training sessions on rollers at the beginning of this period can be very interesting, because of your limited training time. The strength training sessions can be especially helpful, as they give a very high output in spite of the restricted training time available (see below).

This does not mean you can't cycle on the road during your preparation period. However, the longer endurance training sessions with the bicycle are only undertakenwhen the weather conditions improve. These longer training sessions are also best planned in the weekends, when you have more time and can train in a more relaxed way.

It is not our intention to train at the same intensity every week, or to force up your training intensity week by week. Your training set-up should follow a wave-like motion. An excellent system the increasing block-system cycle. This cycle is the best choice for athletes who want to increase their training volume, and not really their training intensity.

The increasing block-system cycle

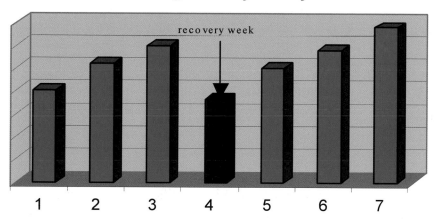

Increasing block-system cycle

recovery week

1   2   3   4   5   6   7

Properties:

- The increase of the training volume goes in a wave-like motion;
- Suitable for forcing up the training quantity;
- The increasing block-system cycle is particularly useful during the second part of the preparation period;
- A test can be carried out at the end of the fourth week;
- Week 1 ‹ week 5, week 2 ‹ week 6, week 3 ‹ week 7
- Week 3 and week 7 are weeks with a high training volume. These weeks are very suitable for planning a large volume of bike training.

The microcycle (week cycle)

In a weekly cycle, a wave-like motion of intensity should also be observed. You avoid training intensively two days in a row.

A more intensive training day is followed by a moderate training day, which is then followed by a relatively light training day.

One day per week is reserved as recovery day. If you are well trained, this generally means a relative recovery day on which you train very quietly (one training session). If you are not yet in excellent shape, you best opt for a recovery day withno training at all.

The week cycle

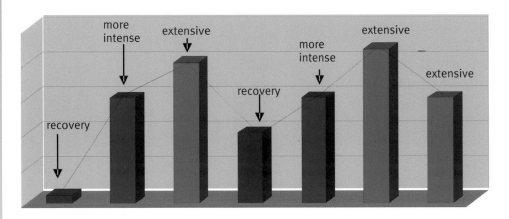

It is important to plan the training sessions well in advance, and develop the plan as you go for the short term. You must know in advance where you want you training to take you.

But your plan should always be flexible. There are always factors, such as weather conditions, illness, fatigue etc. that will spoil the best plan. This means that your training planwill continuously have to be adjusted.

CHAPTER 4

Determining the Intensity of the Training

The key to improving your performance level lies in pairing the type of training you want to pursue with the right training intensity.

In other words, if you want to carry out LSD cycling or run training, you must know exactly how fast (or how slow) you can cycle or run to realize the training impact you want from this kind of training. This type of training specifically aims to stimulate oxidation of fatty acids, among other things. Too high a tempo would, however, stimulate carbohydrate oxidation instead.

In addition, determining the right training intensity is important to stipulating the time needed to reach supercompensation (see below).

You should pay attention to both the quantity of training and the quality (intensity) of training. The intensity can vary from vaguely to very detailed. You can define the quality of a training session as quiet, extensive, recovery training, fartlek, intensive, etc.

You can also express the training intensity using figures, e.g. "up to 80% of maximum", "30 kilometers per hour", "to a heart rate between 170 and 175", "doing a tempo of more or less 2 mmol lactic acid".

Obviously the closer the training intensity and the efficiency come to overlapping, the more effective the training will be.

Generally speaking the most common parameters used to define the training intensity are:
- Subjective feeling (slow, fast, quiet...)
- Heart rate frequency
- Lactic acid concentration in blood

Subjective feeling

Using this parameter you merely trust your gut instinct to determine the intensity of your training. The feeling during the different training forms logically should be the following:

Recovery training and AET1 and AET2

- Comfortable

- You can still continue this tempo easily for a long time

- You breathe easily

- You can easily talk during the effort. As a matter of fact you could tell a complete story without interruptions.

AET3

- Less comfortable feeling
- Tempo is not exactly easy, but nevertheless you can keep it up approximately 30 to 60 minutes
- You breathe more quickly and superficially
- Talking during cycling or running gets more difficult. Only short sentences with interruptions are still possible.

Fartlek

- The feeling during this speed game depends entirely on the quality of the intensive parts. Generally the feeling during the intensive parts is uncomfortable, and talking is difficult.

Threshold training and tempo interval run

- Uncomfortable feeling
- You can keep up the tempo a maximum 10 to 15 minutes
- You breathe rapidly and superficially
- Talking is almost impossible during this kind of training, and you must restrict yourself to pronouncing a few words

High intensity interval training

- Your legs and even your arms feel heavy and painful because of the piling-up of lactic acid in your muscles
- You breath very quickly now
- Talking has become completely impossible, even for a while after finishing

This subjective feeling is an important parameter. Nevertheless you must be careful with your gut instinct. If you feel good, and you are in good shape, there is a risk that the training intensity (continuous) will be too high. Therefore it is advisable to also use other parameters to determine your optimal training intensity.

Heart rate

A commonly used method to determine the training intensity has been based on the heart rate during the effort. This parameter not only provides very important information on the intensity of your training, but also on your level of conditioning.

It is a fact that up to a point, the heart rate increases linearly to the increasing intensity of the training, and therefore comparing heart rates at various times gives a clear picture of the value of the training. Better conditioning translates into a lower heart rate for the same effort.

In other words, if you later notice that you can produce a higher tempo at a lower heart rate, this means that a positive training impact has taken place.

Improved conditioning is also expressed in a more rapid drop to a resting heart rate after the effort.

How can the heart rate be measured?
In the first place you can measure heart rate manually by feeling and counting the heart rate near the heart, the carotid artery or the radial artery. This method is obviously very inaccurate, especially if the heart rate is high and you cannot count immediately after the effort.

Measuring heart rates is most accurate when using a wireless heart rate monitor. Using this method, you can continuously monitor your heart rate during the effort.

Training intensity based on the percentage of the maximum heart rate

You can determine your training intensity based on certain percentages of your maximum heart rate.

After a sound warm-up of at least ten to fifteen minutes ending with tempo accelerations, you can determine your maximum heart rate by cycling or running for one to two minutes at full speed (for cycling preferably uphill). This maximum heart rate can be also determined during a maximum effort test at the doctor.

The maximum heart rate can be also determined by the rule of thumb "220–age". If you are 30 years old, you could conclude that your maximum heart rate is 190 beats per minute. Although this often gets close to the right number, it is best to start from your real maximum heart rate, if possible.

Remember, the maximum heart rate in itself provides absolutely no indication of your condition, and is not due to your training. The maximum heart rate will gradually decrease, however, as you get older.

This method has the advantage that it is very easily determined and useful for training, but a disadvantage is the evolution of the conditioning is not taken into account at all. In other words, independent of your condition, the training heart rates will always be the same since the maximum heart rate does not change due to the influence of training.

Training intensity based on the formula of Karvonen

When calculating training intensity, the formula of Karvonen takes into account the resting heart rate, apart from the maximum heart rate.

% (HR maximum – HR rest) + HR rest = HR during the effort

For example:

Your resting heart rate is 50 and your maximum heart rate is 200. You want to train to 70% of the maximum intensity. The training heart rates are then calculated as follows:

$$0.7 \ (200\text{-}50) + 50 = 155$$

The advantage of the formula of Karvonen is that this formula is applicable to everyone. It is also a reliable method to show a good correlation with the more specialized lactic acid tests.

An additional advantage is that by using this formula the condition of the triathlete is taken into account. As the resting heart rate decreases (better condition), the formula will also produce different results.

Determining the resting heart rate

It is interesting to look at measuring and interpreting the resting heart rate. It's best to measure your resting heart rate lying down, just after awakening. The circumstances for measuring resting heart rate must always be the same.

What can you infer from this?

The resting heart rate gives you an insight into the evolution of your shape

It is common practice that if your shape improves, your resting heart rate decreases. On the other hand, if you train no longer or less often, after a while your resting heart rate will increase.

Your resting heart rate can be considered the barometer of the body

An elevated resting heart rate can be a sign:

- that you have insufficiently recovered from the efforts made, either in a training session, or during a race.

  If you are well trained, an increase of only a few heart beats (about 5% or 10%) obliges you to be careful.

  If you are less well trained, your resting heart rate is more affected by previous training labor. In this case your resting heart rate can be 7 to 10 beats or 15-20% higher before an alarm bell will sound.

  If your resting heart rate is raised, you should insert a rest day or a lighter training session. Continuous attention to the resting heart rate remains necessary.

- of a viral infection such as influenza, before other symptoms appear.

  Less training, or even complete rest, are required to prevent reducing the resistance of your body further against the rising infection. Recovery will be much quicker than if you continue to train, risking a more serious infection and extended illness.

A regular and precise measurement and interpretation of the morning pulse curve can spare you a lot of trouble.

Notes

A low resting heart rate is not an absolute measure of your conditioning. A triathlete having 45 for resting heart rate is not necessarily in better condition than an athlete having a resting heart rate of 50.

Moreover, a low resting heart rate does not always guarantee that your form is optimum (see below).

Factors influencing the heart frequency

If you use the heart rate monitor to determine your training intensity, you should take into account a number of factors, apart from training intensity, that may influence the heart rate.

Illness

If you are ill, you have a (much) higher heart rate than usual, both during rest and during effort. It cannot be stressed too often that training when you are sick is useless and even dangerous. A sick body is not trainable.

Loss of fluids

Loss of fluids increases the heart rate during effort. It is thus very important to drink sufficiently during all training sessions and races.

Altitude

When you go on an altitude-training period, you will see that your heart rate at rest and during efforts is higher than usual.

After an acclimatization period of a few days, the heart rate at rest drops to the normal value. This also is the indicator that training can now be resumed as usual.

However, it is much more difficult to attain the normal maximum heart rate during altitude training.

Medicines

Some medicines have a direct impact on the heart rate.

Nutrition

Eating food full of carbohydrates before training, and drinking energy drinks during training sessions and races, leads to a lower heart rate.

Someone who neglects to replace his carbohydrate stores after high intensity training sessions and races will no longer be able to obtain a high heart rate after a while. This will lead to being overtrained.

Cooling
Cooling during a long-term effort brings along a drop in heart rate.

Stress
During a race, the heart rate is higher than usual, especially for athletes under stress. For these athletes, it is not very useful to wear a heart rate monitor during races, and does not make sense to measure the resting heart rate on the morning of a race.

The muscle mass used
Using more muscle mass during the effort increases the heart rate. That is why it is easier to attain a higher heart rate when cycling uphill than when cycling on a flat track.

Temperature and humidity
The heart rate increases in warm weather and high humidity, both in rest and during efforts. The heart rate reaches its most normal values between 16°C/60°F and 20°C/68°F.

If the temperature is lower than 16°C/60°F, it gets more difficult to reach the heart rate limits for the different types of training. Starting at 12°C/54°F, the heart rate limits can be reduced by one heart rate per degree.

Overtraining
An athlete who is over-trained can no longer reach their maximum heart rate. The heart rate during effort is thus lower than usual, And is sometimes wrongfully interpreted as a positive sign (a lower heart rate for the same effort).

Conclusion:
The heart rate monitor is a very useful instrument to control your training intensity. You must take into account, however, the different factors that can influence your heart rate. The heart rate monitor is most efficient for a triathlete during training segments where you train to a relatively low heart rate.

Lactic acid concentration in blood

A more scientific method to determine your training intensity is determining the lactic acid concentration in your blood during an effort.

At rest, the lactic acid concentration in the blood amounts to 1 to 2 mmol/liter. This lactic acid concentration remains constant as long as the triathlete remains at rest or trains at a moderate intensity. As long as the lactic acid concentration remains stable or only increases slightly, the effort can be continued for a very long time, theoretically speaking, because the lactic acid formed is also being removed during the effort.

As the effort intensity continues to increase, the amoung of lactic acid also starts to increase. As the intensity continues to increase, the lactic acid concentration rises more dramatically, and at high intensity will eventually show a very strong increase curve.

At this moment you will be obliged to stop the effort or to strongly scale back the intensity. For a well-trained triathlete, the cycling, running or swimming speed will be higher before the curve shows a strong increase than for a less well-trained athlete.

By means of laboratory tests, a very precise link can be made between the lactic acid concentration and the capacity of the cyclist, and between the lactic acid concentration and the heart rate.

This test is generally conducted using a gradual effort test on a bicycle ergometer or on a running treadmill. This means that the workload (cycling) or speed (running) is being raised (depending on the test protocol) after a few minutes.

The time span of each effort stage should be at least 4 minutes to attain a constant lactic acid value.

The training recommendation is based on the course of the lactic acid curve. The point where the lactic acid curve shows a strong increase (heart rate 164) is vital. We can conclude that the threshold is situated here.

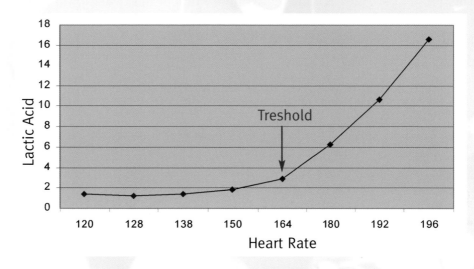

Lactic acid curve

CHAPTER 5

Swimming Training

If you don't have any experience in swimming, this component will undoubtedly be the most difficult discipline to train for. Of the three disciplines, it is the most technical, and moreover it is practical reasons that make it more difficult to train for swimming than running or cycling. Swimming several lengths in a swimming pool crowded with fun-loving people and children playing is often discouraging. Swimming during the quiet mornings or late at night often are the only possible alternatives.

Specific and required training in open water is not so easy either. Cold and dirty water is rather unstimulating.

A lot of triathletes preparing for the Ironman swim more than 15 kilometers per week, even up to a weekly total of 25 kilometers. This is of course much more than required in order to reach the finish. If your goal is to finish within the stipulated times, fewer kilometers will easily do. But you should do a minimum volume of 6 to 8 kilometers a week, divided into two or three training sessions.

Technical training

We will restrict this discussion to the fastest and most effective swimming style, which is the crawl.

A good technical implementation of the crawl is a basic condition necessary to improve your swimming performance. This kind of training is thus the most complex component of triathlon training.

The arm movement

The crawl arm movement can be subdivided into 6 phases: the entry phase, the glide position, the pull phase, the push phase, the exit phase and the recovery phase.

- *The entry phase*
  While entering the water the hand touches the water first by its fingertips, between the top of the shoulder and the longitudinal axis through the body. Thumb and index finger touch the water first. The arm is stretched under water afterwards.

- *The glide position*
  Following entry, the lead arm and shoulder reach forward and then hold a glide position.

- *The pull phase*
  During this phase the arm is bent and because of the inward turning of the upperarm, the hand is taken under the elbow.

  Right before the next phase (push phase) the shoulders, the elbow and the hand are in the same vertical area.

- *The push phase*
  During the push phase the arm is being stretched again. The hand and the lower arm push the water in the direction of the feet.

  During the pull and push phase the wrist follows the longitudinal axis through the body.

- *The exit phase*
  After the push phase the arm is being removed from the water at the height of the thigh, first the shoulder, then the elbow and only at the end the hand.

- *The recovery phase*
  The recovery of the arm is being done using a "high" elbow, and a relaxed hand which remains right above the water.

The leg movement

According to the number of kicks that are being done during one arm cycle, the leg movement (flutter kick) can be subdivided into 2-tact, 4-tact and 6-tact. A 6-tact means that a downward and upward movement using your legs has been done six times per arm cycle.

If you carry out a spurt of 50 meters only using your legs, it will quickly become clear that the flutter kick demands a lot of energy and propels relatively little in comparison with the arm movement. Hence it does not make much sense to do fast leg movements when swimming long distances. The input is much too high in comparison with the output.

2-tact is thus absolutely preferred to 4- or 6-tact for triathlon.
Even more than propelling, the function of the leg movement is to keep the body horizontal, reduce the lateral movements and enable the torso rotation around the longitudinal axis.

The flutter kick starts from the hip, using only a light knee bend, and overstretched feet, which are slightly twisted inward.

Mutual coordination of arms-legs crawl 2-tact

left arm	right arm	left leg	right leg
entry	push	upward	downward
glide position	exit	upward	downward
pull	recovery	upward	downward
push	entry	downward	upward
exit	glide position	downward	upward
recovery	pull	downward	upward

This is a crossed coordination: this means that when the arm goes downward (entry, glide position, pull) the contrary leg as well goes downward.

Breathing

Breathing occurs during the phase glide position – exit. If you breathe on the right side, the glide position of the left arm will help you to hold your mouth above the water for a moment.

In long distance swimming you very often opt for a breathing moment which is repeated every other arm cycle. So you always breathe at the same side. Better swimmers often prefer to breathe every three strokes; they breathe alternatively left and right. Breathing out always happens under water.

Swimming in open water brings about an additional "navigation problem". A look ahead every six to ten arm cycles to locate a buoy or any swimmers ahead is absolutely necessary, possibly made easier when you are able to breathe both left and right.

These two techniques (looking forward and breathing both left and right) must certainly be taken into consideration during swim training.

Main errors, effects and improvement

Error	Consequence	Improvement
Crossing over during entry	Loss of streamline by lateral movements of the pelvis, the result being slowing down	Visual orientation on entry phase (head above water) and overcorrection
Lateral entry of the hand into the water	Loss of streamline by lateral movements of the pelvis, the result being slowing down	Visual orientation on entry phase (head above water) and overcorrection
Catch up: the hand remains too long in the glide position	Swimming in shocks, energy loss	Immediately after the glide position proceed to the pull phase. Pay attention to coordination glide position – exit phase
Lateral pulling and pushing: the hand moves laterally during the pull and push phase	Loss of streamline by lateral movements of the pelvis, the result being slowing down	Visual orientation on the pull and push phase and overcorrection
Crossing over while pulling and pushing: the hand crosses over the longitudinal axis during the pull and push phase	Loss of streamline by lateral movements of the pelvis, the result being slowing down	Visual orientation on the pull and push phase and overcorrection
Slipping through the water, "struggling" with the water push phase: the hand causes turbulence	Short push phase	Use the lower arm to push by twisting the upperarm inwards, position the hand in the direction of the feet during the push phase. Swim with one arm
Exit too early: the hand leaves the water too rapidly at the height of the loins	Loss in push phase	Exit far, position hand in the direction of feet, touch thigh when leaving the water (overcorrection). Swim with one arm
The hand first leaves the water during the exit phase	Disturbing streamline due to pulling the body downward	Remove the elbow from the water, recover with

Error	Consequence	Improvement
		high elbow, ticking armpit (see p. 52) when recovering (overcorrection)
Recovering laterally with a stretched arm: the hand is swayed laterally over the water during recovery phase	Loss of streamline by lateral movements of the pelvis, the result being slowing down	Recovery phase with high elbow, ticking armpit when recovering (overcorrection) let fingertips skate across the water during recovery phase (overcorrection), swim right next to the wall
Too short of a glide position: the arm proceeds from the entry phase immediately to the pull phase	Body rotates too far during breathing, crossing over during the pull and push phase	Catch up
Asymmetric rotation: turning the body excessively to one side	Asymmetric arm movement, loss in push phase, crossing over during the pull and push phase on one side	Breathing every three strokes, both left and right
Scissor movement with the legs: spreading the legs, often due to an asymmetric rotation	Slowing down	Breathing every three strokes, both left and right, crossing over the legs during 2-tact
Swimming with "coat rack" feet: feet are at an angle	Slowing down	Consciously overstretching the foot

It is very difficult to determine your own mistakes and improve them. Therefore it is advisable that you are counseled by a coach with technical knowledge who can give instruction on the edge of the swimming pool.

Even triathletes who swim well should regularly plan the following exercises during the warm-up of their swimming training sessions:

Even triathletes who swim well should regularly plan the following technique exercises during the warm-up for their swim training sessions:

- Ticking the armpit: during recovery touch the armpit with the thumb;

- Gliding: during recovery let the finger tips glide over the water

- Catch up swimming: stay in the glide position until the other hand enters the water.

- Swimming with one arm

- Swimming with your head above the water

- Swimming with clenched fists to use the lower arm as pushing area

- Ticking thigh: at the exit touch the thigh (push out far)

The actual swimming training

Given the restricted time you can spend on this component, it makes little or no sense to train intensively for swimming. It will boil down to training for aerobic endurance through extensive endurance training sessions. Since the swim is still followed by two other disciplines in a triathlon, you should leave the water without any lactic acid piling up in the muscles. This is another important reason to train often at relatively low intensity. A third argument to swim at low intensity is that swimming is an excellent training type to recover from tough training sessions in the two other disciplines.

The most important principles for your swimming training

1. Do technique exercises during warm-up.

2. At the end of the warm-up and right before cooling down, regularly do some climax accelerations during 25 meter laps. This means that you start the 25 meters very slowly, and that you accelerate gradually so you sprint full speed during the last 5 meters.

3. Often swim "progressively". This means that when doing a number of repetitions of long distance, you start slowly and gradually accelerate during the following repetitions.

For example:

- 3x400 meters, progressively from 1 to 3, which means you swim slowly the first 400 meters, the second slightly faster and the third even faster. The last repetition can be done in a "broken swim" (you divide the last repetition into a number of distances) in which the total time is faster than in the previous repetition.

For example:

- 3 x 400:
- 1st 400 meters relaxed
- 2nd 400 meters slightly higher tempo
- 3rd 400 meters: 4x100 meters, in which the total time is faster than the second 400 meters.

4. Only take a short recovery time between the repetitions, especially if you do repetitions over relatively short distances. This short recovery time prevents you from lactic acid piling up during training.

For example:

10 times 100 meters, recovery time 10 seconds

5. Regularly do repetitions over long distances, for example 3 x 800 meters, or even 3 x 1000 meters.

6. Swim as much as possible in a negative split, which means you try to swim faster the second part of the distance than the first part.

7. Vary your tempo during long, uninterrupted swim distances. An excellent means to do this is "locomotion swimming". This means that you alternatively swim a part of the distance slowly, followed by the same distance to a somewhat higher tempo.

For example:

2400 meters locomotion: 100 meters – 200 meters – 300 meters – 300 meters – 200 meters – 100 meters: alternate between relaxed and faster tempo (therefore 100 meters relaxed – 100 meters faster – 200 meters relaxed – 200 meters faster....)

Determining the intensity of swimming training

In swim training it is practically impossible to measure heart rate. In the best case the heart rate can be measured immediately after the effort. During the effort you cannot adjust on the basis of heart rate data. That's why the intensity of training is expressed in swim speed, generally in the form of the tempo in 100 meters.

A good way to set the pace for the different types of swim training consists of adding a certain percentage of your best time at a certain distance to your time. You should first plan a test to see how fast you swim 100, 200 and 400 meters.

Type of training	Distance	Best time + % of this time	Feeling
Recovery	100	+30%	Very relaxed
T1	200	+25%	
	400	+20%	
	Continuous swimming	+25% of best time 400 meters	
AET1	100	+25%	Very relaxed
T2	200	+20%	
	400	+15%	
	Continuous swimming	+20% of best time 400 meters	
AET2	100	+20%	Relaxed
T3	200	+15%	
	400	+10%	
	Continuous swimming	+15% of best time 400 meters	
AET3	100	+15%	Less comfortable feeling
T4	200	+10%	
	400	+8%	
	Continuous swimming	+11% of best time 400 meters	
Tempo training	100	+12%	Tough training
T5	200	+8%	
	400	+6%	
	Continuous swimming	+8% of best time 400 meters	
Anaerobic training	100	+10%	Very tough training
	200	+5%	
T6	400	+4%	
	Continuous swimming	+6% of best time 400 meters	

For example:

Your best time over 100 m is 1:30 , and you want to do an extensive endurance training sesson (AET2) in which you do repetitions of 100 meters (10x100). You will swim every 100 meters to a tempo of 90 sec + 20% = 1:48, with each time a 10 second recovery.

Obviously the first three training types in particular will be taken into consideration in your training set-up. The more intensive training programs would be intended for triathletes who complete a larger training volume.

Examples of the different types of swimming training sessions

After reading the above principles and intensity specifications, you should be able to compose your training set-ups yourself. Nevertheless we provide below some examples for basic set-ups, extensive endurance and intensive endurance.

Explanation of the terms and abbreviations used:

- techn.: technique exercises
- relax: swim in a very relaxed way
- la: left arm
- ra: right arm
- kick: legs
- progr.: swimming progressively
- neg.: swimming with negative split
- 1/3, 1/5: breathe every 3, every 5 strokes
- V: start. V2' means start again every 2 minutes
- p.: paddles
- p.b.: pull buoy
- alt.: alternating
- rec.: recovery time
- ': minutes
- ": seconds

Extensive endurance (T1 to T3)

Extensive endurance 1

- Warming up

    - 200 relax
    - 2x50 techn., rec. 15"
    - 4x25 climax, V.1'
    - 100 relax

- Core

    - 3x200, 1-3, T1-T3, rec. 15"
    - 100 easy
    - 3x200, 1-3, T1-T3, rec.15"
    - 100 easy
    - 3x200, 1-3, T1-T3, rec.15"

- Cooling down

    - 400 relax

Total: 2900 meters

Extensive endurance 2

- Warming up
    - 100 relax
    - 25 la / 25 ra / 25 catch up / 25 ticking armpit
    - 50 relax
    - 4x25 climax, V.1'
    - 100 relax

- Core

    - 3x800
      1) relax, p.+p.b., 1/3
      2) T2 1/3
      3) 4x200 T3, rec. 15"
    - 100 relax

- Cooling down

    - 300 relax

Total: 3100 meters

Extensive endurance 3

- Warming up
  - 100 relax 1/3
  - 200 techn.

- Core

  - 800, faster than intermediate time above, register in-between time 600
  - 600, faster than intermediate time above, register in-between time 400
  - 400, faster than intermediate time above, register in-between time 200
  - 200, faster than intermediate time above
  - 100 relax
  - 4x25 climax, V.1'

- Cooling down

  - 400 relax

Total: 2900 meters

Extensive endurance 4

- Warming up

  - 3x (75 relax-25 climax)
  - 4x50 techn.

- Core

  - 10x100, alt. T1-T2, rec. 15"
  - 100 relax
  - 10x100, alt. T1-T3, rec. 15"
  - 100 relax

- Cooling down

  - 400 relax

Total: 3100 meters

Extensive endurance 5

- Warming up

  - 200 relax
  - 4x50 techn.
  - 100 relax

- Core

  - 2x1000
    1) progressive each 250 (every 250 a little faster)
    2) 4x (200 relax – 50 somewhat higher tempo)

- Cooling down

  - 400 relax

Total: 2900 meters

Extensive endurance 6

- Warming up

  - 200 relax

- Core

  - 2400 locomotion: 100-200-300-300-200-100 alt.
    relax – somewhat higher tempo, first part p. + p.b.

- Cooling down

  - 400 relax

Total: 3000 meters

Extensive endurance 7

- Warming up

  - 200 relax
  - 4x50 techn., rec. 15"
  - 100 relax
  - 3x (50 relax – 25 climax)

- Core

  - 5x400, 1-3/4-5: T1-T3/T1-T3

- Cooling down

  - 400 relax

Total: 3125 meters

Intensive endurance (T4)

Intensive endurance 1

- Warming up
  - 200 relax
  - 4x 25, alt. relax – climax, rec. 15"
  - 100 relax 1/5

- Core
  - 10x100 T3, rec. 10"
  - 100 relax
  - 10x100 T4, rec. 15"

- Cooling down
  - 400 relax

Total: 2900 meters

Intensive endurance 2

- Warming up
  - 100 relax
  - 200 slightly progr. each 50
  - 2x50 techn. Rec. 10"

- Core
  - 3x800
    1) T3 1/5
    2) T4 1/3
    3) 4x200 T4, rec. 15"

- Cooling down
  - 400 relax

Total: 3200 meters

Intensive endurance 3

- Warming up
  - 100 relax
  - 4x50 techn.
  - 2x25 climax, V.1'
  - 2x (12.5 relax – 12.5 sprint), rec. 20"
  - 100 relax
- Core
  - 4x400, 1-2/3-4: T2 – T4/T3 – T4, rec. 30"
  - 100 relax
  - 4x100, total time faster than 5° 400 above, rec. 10"
- Cooling down
  - 400 relax

Total: 3000 meters

Intensive endurance 4

- Warming up
  - 100 relax
  - 4x50 techn., rec.10"
  - 4x (25 relax-25 climax), rec. 15"
  - 100 relax
- Core
  - 4x200 T3, rec. 10"
  - 100 relax
  - 4x200 T4, rec. 15"
  - 100 relax
  - 1x200 T5
- Cooling down
  - 400 relax

Total: 3000 meters

Intensive endurance 5

- Warming up

    - 100 relax
    - 4x (25 relax – 25 climax legs)
    - 100 relax

- Core

    - 800 T3 1/5
    - 100 relax
    - 2x400 T4, rec. 15"
    - 100 relax
    - 4x200 T4, rec. 15"

- Cooling down

    - 400 relax

Total: 3400 meters

Intensive endurance 6

- Warming up

    - 200 relax
    - 4x25 climax, V.1'
    - 100 relax

- Core

    - 4x600:
      1) 200 high tempo – 400 relax
      2) 400 relax – 200 high tempo
      3) 200 high tempo – 200 relax –
         200 high tempo
      4) T4 rec. each time 30"

- Cooling down

    - 400 relax

Total: 3200 meters

Materials

For the swim component a number of very important items are required.

1. **Wetsuit**

   A wetsuit is a neoprene suit that protects you against the cold water. When purchasing this suit you need to keep in mind two important requirements:
   - The suit must fit the body very tightly
   - The suit must be very smooth, especially in the shoulder area so that the arm movement can be done without being hindered.

   Beside the protection against the cold, a wetsuit has another important advantage, especially for the not-so-good swimmers in particular. Your floating capacity strongly improves by wearing a wetsuit.

2. **Swimming goggles**

   Having good swim goggles is extremely important. Make sure they fit well to prevent leaking. First moisten the inner part of the goggles before you put them on, so they will not become steamy during the race.

3. **Towel**

When coming out of the water you often run across sand or grass towards your bike. Have a towel ready next to your bicycle, so that you can rub the sand off your feet before you put on your cycling shoes.

4. **Sunblock**

If you compete in a race in warm and sunny conditions, you can best apply waterproof sun lotion before the swim. In very sunny conditions you can use your sun lotion once more on your neck and arms right before you leave on your bike, just to be sure you are well protected.

CHAPTER 6

Bike Training

Experience teaches us that the two disciplines for which people train best and most efficiently are swimming and running. That's why especially swimming and running coaches are responsible for the high flight triathlon has taken in terms of performance enhancement.

Specific bike training is, on the other hand, being neglected by a lot of triathletes. They do cycle a lot, but in most of the cases very little professionally, and the other athletes they train with mostly determines the training intensity.

As mentioned before, you should specifically train the aerobic zone.

Determining the intensity of bike training

The heart rate areas for the different training programs can be inferred from the next table:

Training intensity cycling based on the percentage of the maximum heart rate

Nature of training	% of the maximum heart frequency
Recovery training	- 65%
AET1	66-68%
AET2	69-72%
AET3	73-82%
Threshold training on a flat track	83-86%
Threshold training uphill	87-90%
High Intensity interval training	+ 90%

Training intensity based on the formula of Karvonen

Based on the formula of Karvonen, the heart rate areas for the different training programs can be calculated as follows:

Type of training	% of the maximum capacity
Recovery training	- 60%
AET1	61-64%
AET2	65-70%
AET3	71-78%
Threshold training on a flat track	79-81%
Threshold training uphill	82-84%
Submaximal interval training	85-89%
High intensity interval training	+90%

Elaborated example:

Maximum heart rate = 200
Heart rate at rest = 50

- Recovery training: $0.60 \ (200\text{-}50) +50 = 140$

- AET1 $0.61 \ (200\text{-}50) +50 = 141$
     $0.64 \ (200\text{-}50) +50 = 146$

- AET2 $0.65 \ (200\text{-}50) +50 = 147$
     $0.70 \ (200\text{-}50) +50 = 155$

- AET3 $0.71 \ (200\text{-}50) +50 = 156$
     $0.78 \ (200\text{-}50) +50 = 167$

- Threshold flat track $0.79 \ (200\text{-}50) +50 = 168$
     $0.81 \ (200\text{-}50) +50 = 172$

- Threshold uphill $0.82 \ (200\text{-}50) +50 = 173$
     $0.84 \ (200\text{-}50) +50 = 176$

- Submax. interval training $0.85 \ (200\text{-}150) +50 = 177$
     $0.89 \ (200\text{-}50) +50 = 184$

- High int. interval training $+0.90 \ (200\text{-}50) +50 = 185$

Lower limit heart rate AET1

Hr/Hm	205	200	195	190	185	180	175	170
35	137	134	131	128	125	122	119	116
40	139	136	133	130	127	124	121	118
45	141	138	135	132	129	126	123	120
50	143	140	137	134	131	128	125	122
55	145	142	139	136	133	130	127	124
60	147	144	141	138	135	132	129	126
65	149	146	143	140	137	134	131	128
70	151	148	145	142	139	136	133	130
75	153	150	147	144	141	138	135	132
80	155	152	149	146	143	140	137	134

Upper limit heart rate AET1

Hr/Hm	205	200	195	190	185	180	175	170
35	144	141	137	134	131	128	125	121
40	146	142	139	136	133	130	126	123
45	147	144	141	138	135	131	128	125
50	149	146	143	140	136	133	130	127
55	151	148	145	141	138	135	132	129
60	153	150	146	143	140	137	134	130
65	155	151	148	145	142	139	135	132
70	156	153	150	147	144	140	137	134
75	158	155	152	149	145	142	139	136
80	160	157	154	150	147	144	141	138

Lower limit heart rate AET2

Hr/Hm	205	200	195	190	185	180	175	170
35	144	141	137	134	131	128	125	121
40	146	142	139	136	133	130	126	123
45	147	144	141	138	135	131	128	125
50	149	146	143	140	136	133	130	127
55	151	148	145	141	138	135	132	129
60	153	150	146	143	140	137	134	130
65	155	151	148	145	142	139	135	132
70	156	153	150	147	144	140	137	134
75	158	155	152	149	145	142	139	136
80	160	157	154	150	147	144	141	138

Upper limit heart rate AET2

Hr/Hm	205	200	195	190	185	180	175	170
35	154	151	147	144	140	137	133	130
40	156	152	149	145	142	138	135	131
45	157	154	150	147	143	140	136	133
50	159	155	152	148	145	141	138	134
55	160	157	153	150	146	143	139	136
60	162	158	155	151	148	144	141	137
65	163	160	156	153	149	146	142	139
70	165	161	158	154	151	147	144	140
75	166	163	159	156	152	149	145	142
80	168	164	161	157	154	150	147	143

Lower limit heart rate AET3

Hr/Hm	205	200	195	190	185	180	175	170
35	154	151	147	144	140	137	133	130
40	156	152	149	145	142	138	135	131
45	157	154	150	147	143	140	136	133
50	159	155	152	148	145	141	138	134
55	160	157	153	150	146	143	139	136
60	162	158	155	151	148	144	141	137
65	163	160	156	153	149	146	142	139
70	165	161	158	154	151	147	144	140
75	166	163	159	156	152	149	145	142
80	168	164	161	157	154	150	147	143

Upper limit heart rate AET3

Hr/Hm	205	200	195	190	185	180	175	170
35	168	164	160	156	152	148	144	140
40	169	165	161	157	153	149	145	141
45	170	166	162	158	154	150	146	143
50	171	167	163	159	155	151	148	144
55	172	168	164	160	156	153	149	145
60	173	169	165	161	158	154	150	146
65	174	170	166	163	159	155	151	147
70	175	171	168	164	160	156	152	148
75	176	173	169	165	161	157	153	149
80	178	174	170	166	162	158	154	150

Lower limit heart rate "threshold training on flat road"

Hr/Hm	205	200	195	190	185	180	175	170
35	168	164	160	156	152	148	144	140
40	169	165	161	157	153	149	145	141
45	170	166	162	158	154	150	146	143
50	171	167	163	159	155	151	148	144
55	172	168	164	160	156	153	149	145
60	173	169	165	161	158	154	150	146
65	174	170	166	163	159	155	151	147
70	175	171	168	164	160	156	152	148
75	176	173	169	165	161	157	153	149
80	178	174	170	166	162	158	154	150

Upper limit heart rate "threshold training on flat road"

Hr/Hm	205	200	195	190	185	180	175	170
35	173	169	165	161	157	152	148	144
40	174	170	166	162	157	153	149	145
45	175	171	167	162	158	154	150	146
50	176	172	167	163	159	155	151	147
55	177	172	168	164	160	156	152	148
60	177	173	169	165	161	157	153	149
65	178	174	170	166	162	158	154	150
70	179	175	171	167	163	159	155	151
75	180	176	172	168	164	160	156	152
80	181	177	173	169	165	161	157	153

Lower limit heart rate "threshold training uphill"

Hr/Hm	205	200	195	190	185	180	175	170
35	173	169	165	161	157	152	148	144
40	174	170	166	162	157	153	149	145
45	175	171	167	162	158	154	150	146
50	176	172	167	163	159	155	151	147
55	177	172	168	164	160	156	152	148
60	177	173	169	165	161	157	153	149
65	178	174	170	166	162	158	154	150
70	179	175	171	167	163	159	155	151
75	180	176	172	168	164	160	156	152
80	181	177	173	169	165	161	157	153

Upper limit heart rate "threshold training uphill"

Hr/Hm	205	200	195	190	185	180	175	170
35	178	174	169	165	161	157	153	148
40	179	174	170	166	162	158	153	149
45	179	175	171	167	163	158	154	150
50	180	176	172	168	163	159	155	151
55	181	177	173	168	164	160	156	152
60	182	178	173	169	165	161	157	152
65	183	178	174	170	166	162	157	153
70	183	179	175	171	167	162	158	154
75	184	180	176	172	167	163	159	155
80	185	181	177	172	168	164	160	156

Lower limit heart rate "submaximal interval training"

Hr/Hm	205	200	195	190	185	180	175	170
35	178	174	169	165	161	157	153	148
40	179	174	170	166	162	158	153	149
45	179	175	171	167	163	158	154	150
50	180	176	172	168	163	159	155	151
55	181	177	173	168	164	160	156	152
60	182	178	173	169	165	161	157	152
65	183	178	174	170	166	162	157	153
70	183	179	175	171	167	162	158	154
75	184	180	176	172	167	163	159	155
80	185	181	177	172	168	164	160	156

Upper limit heart rate "submaximal interval training"

Hr/Hm	205	200	195	190	185	180	175	170
35	186	182	177	173	169	164	160	155
40	187	182	178	174	169	165	160	156
45	187	183	179	174	170	165	161	156
50	188	184	179	175	170	166	161	157
55	189	184	180	175	171	166	162	157
60	189	185	180	176	171	167	162	158
65	190	185	181	176	172	167	163	158
70	190	186	181	177	172	168	163	159
75	191	186	182	177	173	168	164	160
80	191	187	182	178	173	169	165	160

Training priorities

Your rather restricted time to train forces you to set certain priorities for your bike training. First of all, training on rollers will be very important. You get a high output within a short period, you can do this kind of training at any moment of the day and most important, you train when the weather conditions do not allow training outdoors. In addition, you can use very specific training sessions for very efficient suppleness and strength training.

You obviously still need to cycle on the road as well. You can only prepare for the 180 kilometer cycling component of an Ironman race if you train a certain minimum volume. You must be able to dismount your bike sufficiently fit, since a difficult closing marathon awaits you! The fact that drafting is not allowed actually means that you must prepare yourself for a very long time trial. This has additional consequences on your training.

Strength training for cycling

Strength development for cycling can be obtained in two different ways. The first is to train with weights in the gym, and the other to train specifically on the bike. Since the total training time is limited, and we should strive for maximum output in minimum time, we will restrict ourselves to specific strength training on the bicycle.

Specific strength training means the strength training on the bicycle, cycling on an ergometer bicycle or on rollers having adjustable resistance. The greatest difficulty in this kind of specific training is finding the correct resistance.

This resistance is providedby the triathlete, who is always sitting on the saddle, pushing hard to make 40 to 60 rotations per minute (RPM). But you must not exceed the threshold during this training. It demands some experience and searching before specific strength training is carried out correctly.

Number of rotations per minute

Concerning the number of rotations per minute during strength training, opinions differ greatly. One point of view keeps it on 60 RPM. More rotations would hardly be strength training, and less rotations would be too non-specific, i.e. too far removed from reality. Another point of view opts for 40 RPM, because this would allow better recovery after training.

Training set-up

This kind of training can put considerable strain on your knee tendons. That is why you should build up the training workload very gradually.

Strength training on rollers always starts with a warm-up of at least 15 minutes, in which you cycle at 100-120 RPM. You then cycle for a short period at a high gear ratio, 40 or 60 RPM, followed by a short recovery period. During these recovery periods you cycle relaxed at a high pedaling frequency and low heart rate.

week	duration (minutes)	repetitions	recovery (minutes)
1	2	3	2
2	2	4	2
3	3	3	2
4	3	4	2
5	3	5	2
6	3	6	3
7	3	7	3
8	3	8	3
9	4	6	3

It is recommended to smoothly cycle 30 to 60 minutes on the rollers with a low gear ratio or 1 to 2 hours on the road.

> **Note:**
> Take care when you change your bicycle, pedals and shoes. You should strive for a position as close to identical as possible to the your old bicycle position. This generally is possible. The transfer to new shoes and pedals is most difficult.
>
> This change must be gradual, i.e. you cannot train immediately at full strength with the new gear. Possibly you should alternate with the familiar material in the beginning. You should be especially careful with the specific strength training. To avoid injuries you must be adapted for 100% to the new gear before you start this kind of training.

Change of bicycle position must always be very gradual. If you decide to raise your saddle even 1 cm, this must be done progressively, each time in stages of a maximum 3 mm.

Suppleness training

It is advisable to pay some attention to suppleness during a race. Choose your gear ratio so you can cycle at a relatively high pedaling frequency; at least 90 RPM, preferably 100 RPM or more. The advantage of a high pedaling frequency is that you work your cardio-vascular system, and spare your leg muscles. This will help you start running with fit legs. You should cycle at a low gear ratio, especially during the last part of the cycling component, to prepare you best for the running component to come.

Professional cyclists also do their time trials with a high pedaling frequency. During attempts to improve on the hour record, they generally cycle at 100 to 105 RPM. At time trials on the road they also ride at a high pedaling frequency.

Suppleness training on rollers is preferably done on fixed rollers having adjustable resistance; this means that the bicycle is attached to the roller system. This allows safe cycling with a very high pedaling frequency.

This system is really preferable to the stationary bike, because it is very important that you adopt your normal cycling position during this training.

Cycling on rollers

It is useful to assemble a pedaling frequency meter onto your bicycle, so that you always know how fast you are pedaling.

You should learn to cycle with a high pedaling frequency without "shocking" on your bicycle. During these training sessions make sure that you continue to sit firmly on the saddle and that your torso moves as little as possible.

During training you progressively force up the number of rotations until you reach a level you can handle without shocking on your saddle.

The resistance of the roller system remains low. The aim of this kind of training is certainly not anaerobic training. With the low resistance you must be able to keep your heart rate under the threshold pulse, in spite of a very high pedaling frequency.

Time trial training

During an Ironman distance race drafting is forbidden. You will thus be on your own during 180 kilometer cycling track.

First, you must be physically strong enough to be able to ride such a long time trial. You must also be mentally strong to keep focused during 180 kilometers – not only on the race and your competitors, but also, – and especially – on yourself. You should constantly explore your own limits, sense whether the tempo is too high, whether you can still accelerate.

You must also be able to save energy all along the way for the long and hard marathon. Often you ride a solitary race. Your only point of reference is your own training experience, which has taught you which tempo you can maintain during this long cycling component. You must also remain focused on your fluid and food intake during the bike, which lasts for hours.

In short, you must be specifically and well trained to be able to finish this component successfully, and at no time can you allow your focus to slacken.

Technical approach

During an Ironman distance, phenomenal performances have happened during the cycling component. Take Thomas Hellriegel, for example. In 1996, during the Ironman of Hawaii, he rode an average of more than 40 kilometers per hour (4 hours 24 min and 50 sec), and this on a hilly track consistently pestered by heat and wind.

Jürgen Zäck, Pauli Kiuri, Mark Allen, Cristian Bustos, Faris Al-Sultan and Tornbjorn Sindballe as well rode quicker than 40 kilometers per hour in Kona. This is a performance from which even a well-trained professional cyclist might back away.

The reasons for these fantastic performances are not only to be found in perfected training methods and better medical support, but also in the evolution in materials (bicycle) and the position on the bicycle.

Time trial is a technical discipline, in which you must try and do all that is possible to overcome a number of opposing forces. The choice of the material, the bicycle attire and the position on the bicycle are vitally important to overcome these forces.

These opposing forces are: the friction caused by pedals, pedal bracket, chain and derailleur; the rolling resistance; air friction and gravity force.

Technical tips for races in which drafting is not allowed

- Adjust the position on the bicycle so that the frontal surface becomes as small as possible. This can be done by bending the torso forward, keeping the head down as much as possible during the time trial, and keeping the elbows near each other. This certainly gets easier when using triathlon bars. Of course, you have to find a good aerodynamic position which you can maintain comfortably for several hours.

  This requires long training sessions in which race conditions are being simulated, and in which this aerodynamic position is trained at race speed. You must not forget that after finishing the cycling component you have to start a marathon. You can therefore not afford to get a backache during cycling.

- Wear a tight-fitting triathlon suit or tank top.

- Wear an aerodynamic helmet.

- Ride with narrow, firmly pumped tires. When choosing tires take the nature of the road surface into account.

- Ride using a disk wheel if there is little wind and on a flat track. In case of wind and time trials, including climbing, three or four spoke wheels are preferred to disk wheels.

- Ride a light bicycle with flat, oval tubes.

Note:

Fluid intake is very important during a triathlon, especially the *Ironman* distance. You must take along sufficient stock. Beside two drinking bottles (75 cl) which can be taken along in the holders assembled to the framework, two additional drinking bottles are often taken along in a holder attached behind the saddle.

You must, however, take into account that, especially on a hilly track, these bottles bring along an extra weight of 3 kilograms. The bottles behind the saddle also strongly disturb the ideal streamline. If possible, try to confine yourself to 2 bottles, which can be taken along in the traditional holders.

Basic set-ups cycling training

Phase 1: General preparation period

- Training on rollers 60': strength + suppleness

- Training on rollers 60': strength + suppleness

- Long Slow Distance: 120'

Phase 2: Specific preparation period

- Training on rollers 60': strength + suppleness

- Training on rollers 60': strength + suppleness

- AET2 : 120'

- Long Slow Distance: 120' to 300'

CHAPTER 7

Run training

Run training undoubtedly is the most physically straining component of triathlon training. A wrong training set-up, either volume or intensity not only endangers the conditioning of the athlete, but also strongly increases the risk of overload injuries.

The run performance in a triathlon is determined by several factors. First is the specific degree of training by the triathlete. Generally speaking the better runner will also accomplish a better running time in a triathlon.

A second factor – perhaps just as important as the first – is the degree of fitness at the start of the run. A good runner who gets off his bike exhausted will probably have a slower running time than an average runner who starts the run feeling strong and fit. This means that cycling ability strongly contributes to the final run performance!

To run well in a triathlon, you not only need to be well-trained as a runner, but also be well-trained in cycling, and to be able to judge your cycling ability correctly.

Choosing running shoes

As mentioned before, run training is the most physical straining component of triathlon training. You first should be sure you have the correct running shoes.

The choice isn't simple, because the ideal running shoe for every runner does not necessarily exist. The market is constantly being swamped with new models and technical upgrades. Some of these revolutionary upgrades disappear just as quickly as they appear, while others stand the test of time. It has become more and more difficult to see the forest for the trees, and all of us are at risk of making a wrong purchase, possibly causing all sorts of painful impacts.

Most important, a good running shoe must be **shock absorbing**. Your feet, knees, hips and back must cope with a great deal of shock during running. On average, even when running calmly, the pressure on the feet amounts to three to four times your body weight. No wonder that the risk for overload injuries is always lurking for runners.

A good running shoe must also **stabilize** the foot and **neutralize** as many deviations as possible from the normal foot.
Not everyone has a normal foot, and not everyone puts down their foot in the same way when running.

A lot of runners tend to have **flat feet**. This means that the middle of the foot has sagged, to some extent. When making an impression of the foot sole, a flat foot will leave a large, broad impression, in the worse cases even a complete foot sole with no indication of an instep.

Then there are runners with **hollow feet**, where the middle of the foot rises high (high instep). An impression of the foot sole will mostly show the outer edges of the foot sole.

Runners don't all put down their foot the same way either.

In **normal circumstances** you put down the foot on the outside of the heel. When the complete weight comes above the foot, the foot will slightly "unroll" to the inside and in the direction of your big toe. This natural unrolling of the foot is called **normal pronation**, which ensures maximum shock absorption.

After a while, the running shoes for these runners will wear out where they hit the ground first, at the outer parts of the heel. There is also symmetrical wear at the front of the foot, because the foot pushes off using the flat front foot.

Some runners, however, touch the ground first with the inner parts of the foot. The foot unrolls too far to the inside, which places their weight on the inner ankle. This is called **overpronation**. In this case the sole of the shoe will show wear at the inner parts of the sole.

Oversupination, on the other hand, is when the shock as the foot hits the ground is mainly being absorbed by the outside of the foot. The foot unrolls too little to the inside. After a while the complete outer side of the sole will show a lot of wear, because you don't only land on the side of the heel, but you also push away with the outside of the foot.

Either way, it should be clear that you really need specialized advice to choose the correct running shoe.

The correct shoe size

After choosing the correct shoe type, choosing the correct shoe size is very important, too. Shoes that are too large will quickly cause blisters due to the constant movement of the foot in the shoe.

Instead, some triathletes tend to buy their running shoes too small. "A running shoe must fit like a glove" is an expression commonly used in the running world. But you do need to be careful not to buy shoes that are too small. Shoes that are too small feel very uncomfortable, and quickly cause painful, blue toenails. After some time these toenails get loose, and eventually drop off. Loose toenails do not feel comfortable at night in between the sheets ...

You must be certain there is one cm space (more or less) between the big toe and the end of the shoe.

Check the width of the shoe as well. A running shoe should be snug on the side of the heel. At the height of the instep the shoe cannot be too tight under any circumstances.

Also check the suppleness of the sole. The sole should be able to bend sufficiently at the ball of the foot. Soles that are too stiff cause pressure on the plantar fascia, and can cause inflammation of this fascia (plantar fasciitis).

The life span of running shoes

The life span of a shoe mostly depends on the quality of the shoe and on the training surface. Triathletes who typically train on a hardened surface wear out their running shoes faster than triathletes who train on a soft surface.

The care which is given to the running shoes after the training session is also very important. The shoes must be dry and all mud should be removed before running again.

Ideally, you should have two pairs of running shoes, so you can switch shoes for every other training session.

If being well maintained, good running shoes can last up to 1500 kilometers.

Determining the intensity of run training sessions

Training heart rates based on % of the maximum heart rate

Type of training	% of the maximum heart frequency
Recovery training	- 70%
AET1 (Long Slow Distance)	71-75%
AET2	76-80%
AET3	81-87%
Tempo interval training	88-90%
Intensive interval training	+ 90%

Training heart rates based on the formula of Karvonen

Type of training	% of the maximum capacity
Recovery training	- 65%
AET1 (Long Slow Distance)	66-72%
AET2	73-76%
AET3	77-84%
Tempo interval training	85-90%
Intensive interval training	+90%

Lower limit heart rates AET1 according to the Karvonen formula

Hr/Hm	205	200	195	190	185	180	175	170
35	146	142	139	136	133	129	126	123
40	147	144	141	138	134	131	128	125
45	149	146	143	139	137	133	130	126
50	151	148	144	141	138	135	131	128
55	153	149	146	143	140	136	133	130
60	154	151	148	145	141	138	135	132
65	156	153	150	146	143	140	137	133
70	158	155	151	148	145	142	138	135
75	160	156	153	150	147	143	140	137
80	161	158	155	152	148	145	142	139

Upper limit heart rates AET1 according to the Karvonen formula

Hr/Hm	205	200	195	190	185	180	175	170
35	157	154	150	147	143	139	136	132
40	159	155	152	148	144	141	137	134
45	160	157	153	149	146	142	139	135
50	162	158	154	151	147	144	140	136
55	163	159	156	152	149	145	141	138
60	164	161	157	154	150	146	143	139
65	166	162	159	155	151	148	144	141
70	167	164	160	156	153	149	146	142
75	169	165	161	158	154	151	147	143
80	170	166	163	159	156	152	148	145

Lower limit heart rates AET2 according to the Karvonen formula

Hr/Hm	205	200	195	190	185	180	175	170
35	159	155	152	148	145	141	137	134
40	160	157	153	150	146	142	139	135
45	162	158	155	151	147	144	140	136
50	163	160	156	152	149	145	141	138
55	165	161	157	154	150	146	143	139
60	166	162	159	155	151	148	144	140
65	167	164	160	156	153	149	145	142
70	169	165	161	158	154	150	147	143
75	170	166	163	159	155	152	148	144
80	171	168	164	160	157	153	149	146

Upper limit heart rates AET2 according to the Karvonen formula

Hr/Hm	205	200	195	190	185	180	175	170
35	164	160	157	153	149	145	141	138
40	165	162	158	154	150	146	143	139
45	167	163	159	155	151	148	144	140
50	168	164	160	156	153	149	145	141
55	169	165	161	158	154	150	146	142
60	170	166	163	159	155	151	147	144
65	171	168	164	160	156	152	149	145
70	173	169	165	161	157	154	150	146
75	174	170	166	162	159	155	151	147
80	175	171	167	164	160	156	152	148

Lower limit heart AET3 according to the Karvonen formula

Hr/Hm	205	200	195	190	185	180	175	170
35	166	162	158	154	151	147	143	139
40	167	163	159	156	152	148	144	140
45	168	164	161	157	153	149	145	141
50	169	166	162	158	154	150	146	142
55	171	167	163	159	155	151	147	144
60	172	168	164	160	156	152	149	145
65	173	169	165	161	157	154	150	146
70	174	170	166	162	159	155	151	147
75	175	171	167	164	160	156	152	148
80	176	172	169	165	161	157	153	149

Upper limit heart AET3 according to the Karvonen formula

Hr/Hm	205	200	195	190	185	180	175	170
35	178	174	169	165	161	157	153	148
40	179	174	170	166	162	158	153	149
45	179	175	171	167	163	158	154	150
50	180	176	172	168	163	159	155	151
55	181	177	173	168	164	160	156	152
60	182	178	173	169	165	161	157	152
65	183	178	174	170	166	162	157	153
70	183	179	175	171	167	162	158	154
75	184	180	176	172	167	163	159	155
80	185	181	177	172	168	164	160	156

Lower limit heart rates tempo interval training according to the Karvonen formula

Hr/Hm	205	200	195	190	185	180	175	170
35	180	175	171	167	163	158	154	150
40	180	176	172	168	163	159	155	151
45	181	177	173	168	164	160	156	151
50	182	178	173	169	165	161	156	152
55	183	178	174	170	166	161	157	153
60	183	179	175	171	166	162	158	154
65	184	180	176	171	167	163	159	154
70	185	181	166	172	168	164	159	155
75	186	181	177	173	169	164	160	156
80	186	182	178	174	169	165	161	157

Upper limit heart rates tempo interval training according to the Karvonen formula

Hr/Hm	205	200	195	190	185	180	175	170
35	188	184	179	175	170	166	161	157
40	189	184	180	175	171	166	162	157
45	189	185	180	176	171	167	162	158
50	190	185	181	176	172	167	163	158
55	190	186	181	177	172	168	163	159
60	191	186	182	177	173	168	164	159
65	191	187	182	178	173	169	164	160
70	192	187	183	178	174	169	165	160
75	192	188	183	179	174	170	165	161
80	193	188	184	179	175	170	166	161

Training priorities

The aim of run training in preparation for the Ironman distance is to make the aerobic endurance basis as broad as possible and raise the running tempo as high as possible based on your fat metabolism. The most appropriate means to achieve this are Long Slow Distance training sessions. You should mostly train "extensively."

This does not mean that you always run around the same heart rate. In the beginning phase, the intensification of the training volume to low intensity (66-72% according to Karvonen) should be your primary aim. Later in the specific period you can do tempo changes during AET1 sessions, within a 77% and 84% heart rate zone (according to the formula of Karvonen).

The longest Long Slow Distance sessions amount to about 20 to 25 kilometers. Longer distances are not suitable, because the strain on the body will negatively influence the conditioning curve, and the risk of overload injuries really gets too high for a lot of athletes.

Towards the end of the preparation period, you should strive for a training volume of 40-50 kilometers a week. This is a must if you want to finish the longest competitive races.

Tempo of AET1 (LSD) training sessions

You run to a tempo that corresponds to an intensity of 66-72% according to Karvonen. Later you can, even during the longest training sessions, raise the tempo instinctively to 76% according to Karvonen.

Endurance training with tempo changes

During an AET2 session from 45 to 60 minutes, a number of tempo changes of approximately 4 to 6 minutes can be inserted.

The tempo to which you then run corresponds to the AET3 tempo according to the formula of Karvonen.

Example
- 15 min. easy tempo, heart rate 66-72% according to Karvonen
- 4 x 4 min. heart rate 77-84% according to Karvonen, rec. 3 min easy tempo, heart rate 66-72% according to Karvonen
- 15 min. easy tempo, heart rate 72-76% according to Karvonen
- total: 55 minutes

Basic running programs

Phase 1: General preparation period

- 30' recovery

- 30'-45' AET2

- 45'-60' AET1

Phase 2: Specific preparation period

- 45' – 60' AET2

- 45' – 60' AET2, including tempos AET3

- 60' – 120' AET1

Transition training

Transition training is combined swim and bike training, and combined cycling and run training.

It is indeed not always that easy to process the transition between two different disciplines smoothly.

The transition of cycling to running in particular tends to be uncomfortable. That is why you need to train for this transition very specifically.

You can already start this rather early in the preparation phase.

Progression to adopt during this kind of training:

Cycling distance	Running distance	Example
short	short	60 min cycling quietly, followed by 5 to 10 min running in a very relaxed way
short	longer	see above, force up running to 20 to 30 min
longer	longer	120 min cycling, followed by 20 to 30 min running
long	long	120 to 240 min cycling, followed by 30 to 60 min running

A last progression consists of forcing up the cycling tempo towards the end.

CHAPTER 8

24 Week Sample Planner for the Ironman Distance

The training program below has not developed for semi-professional and professional athletes. It is, however, the minimum set-up which should be completed to be able to finish an Ironman. The majority of the training sessions are, of course, planned during weekends.

Guidelines for the set-up of this training planning

1. The set-ups follow a wave-like motion according to the increasing block-system cycle. The training is forced up every three weeks, followed by a relative recovery week.

2. **Swimming:**
   - Two swim training session are done each week
   - Technique exercises are very important during the warm-up
   - During the first eight weeks the training sessions exclusively remain within the T1 – T3 intensity area
   - From the third cycle of three weeks (ninth week), intensity is forced up during one of the two training sessions, to maximum T4
   - During the last weeks in the core of the training, you complete the race distance a couple of times.

3. **Cycling:**
   - During the first 9 weeks, two of the three bike training sessions are done on rollers. From the third week the specific strength training on rollers is taken into consideration.
   - From the third cycle of three weeks (ninth week) you only train on the road
   - The training sessions on the road stay exclusively in the aerobic zone
   - You do at most three bike training sessions per week
   - During the last eight weeks the longest bike training sessions are forced up to more than 240 min

4. **Running:**
   - Because of the risk of overload injuries, the set-up of the run training sessions is very gradual
   - You exclusively train in the aerobic zone
   - From the fourth cycle of three weeks (thirteenth week), longer run training sessions of 90 min and more are taken into consideration.

5. **Transition training**
   - From the fourth cycle of three weeks (thirteenth week) the transition of cycling to running is being trained.

24-Week-Plan

Week 1

Day	Swimming	Cycling	Running
Monday		30' easy on rollers	
Tuesday			40' AET1
Wednesday	**Warm up** • 200m easy • 200m techn. **Core** • 4x400m, alt. T1 – T2, rec. 30" **Cool down** • 400 easy **Total: 2400m**		
Thursday			30' AET2
Friday		30' easy on rollers	
Saturday	**Warm up** • 200m easy • 4x25m climax • 100m easy **Core** • 2x800m, 1-2: T1 – T2, rec. 1' **Cool down** • 400m easy **Total: 2400m**	90' LSD	
Sunday			50' AET1
TOTAL	4800m	150 min	120 min

TOTAL   **6h 10 min.**

Week 2

Day	Swimming	Cycling	Running
Monday		45' easy on rollers	
Tuesday			45' AET1
Wednesday	**Warm up** • 200m easy • 2x25m catch-up • 100m techn. **Core** • 4x200m, alt. T1 – T2, rec.15" • 100m relax • 4x200m, alt. T2 – T3, rec. 30" **Cool down** • 400m easy Total: 2450m		
Thursday			30' AET2
Friday		45' easy on rollers	
Saturday	**Warm up** • 2x (175m relax – 25m climax) • 100m techn. **Core** • 800m T1, rec. 30" • 600m T2, rec. 30" • 400m T3 **Cool down** • 300m easy Total: 2600m	90' LSD	
Sunday			55' AET1
TOTAL	5050m	180 min	130 min
TOTAL	**6h 45 min**		

Day	Swimming	Cycling	Running
Monday		**Spec. strength on rollers** • 15' easy • 3x2' high resistance, 40-60 rpm, rec. 3' easy • 15' easy **Total: 42'**	
Tuesday			50' AET1
Wednesday	**Warm up** • 4x (75m relax-25m climax) • 200m techn. **Core** • 1x800m, T2 • 100m relax • 8x100m, alt. T1 – T3, rec. 10" **Cool down** • 400m easy **Total: 2700m**		
Thursday			35' AET2
Friday		**Spec. strength on rollers** • 15' easy • 3x2' high resistance, 40-60 rpm, rec. 3' easy • 15' easy **Total: 42'**	
Saturday	**Warm up** • 200m easy • 4x (25m relax-25m climax) • 100m easy **Core** • 10x100m, T2, rec. 10" • 100m easy • 5x200m, T3, rec. 15" **Cool down** • 300m easy **Total: 2900m**	120'LSD	
Sunday			60' AET1
TOTAL	5600 m	204 min	145 min

TOTAL	**7h 50 min**

Week 4: recovery

Day	Swimming	Cycling	Running
Monday			
Tuesday			
Wednesday		Spec. strength on rollers • 15' easy • 4x2' high resistance, 40-60 rpm, rec. 3' easy • 15' easy Total: 47'	
Thursday			40' AET2
Friday		Spec. strength on rollers • 15' easy • 4x2' high resistance, 40-60 rpm, rec. 3' easy • 15' easy Total: 47'	
Saturday	Warm up • 200m easy • 4x25m climax • 100m easy Core • 1500 cont. swimming, T2 Cool down • 400m easy Total: 2300m		60' AET1
Sunday		90' LSD	
TOTAL	2300m	184 min	100 min

TOTAL   5h 30 min

Day	Swimming	Cycling	Running
Monday		**Spec. strength on rollers** • 15' easy • 4x3' high resistance, 40-60 rpm, rec. 3' easy • 15' easy **Total: 51'**	
Tuesday			40' AET1
Wednesday	**Warm up** • 200m relax • 2x50m techn., rec. 15" • 4x25m climax, V.1' • 100m relax **Core** • 3x200m, 1-3, T1-T3, rec. 15" • 100 easy • 3x200m, 1-3, T1-T3, rec.15" • 100 easy • 3x200m, 1-3, T1-T3, rec. 15" **Cool down** • 400m easy **Total: 2900m**		
Thursday			30' AET2
Friday		**Spec. strength on rollers** • 15' easy • 4x3 high resistance, 40-60 rpm, rec. 3' easy • 15' easy **Total: 51'**	
Saturday	**Warm up** • 200m easy • 8x25m techn., rec. 15" • 100m relax	90' LSD	

Day	Swimming	Cycling	Running
	Core • 2x400m, 1-2: T2–T3, rec. 30" • 100m easy • 4x200m, 1-2/3-4: T2-T3/T2-T3, rec. 15" • 100m easy • 4x100m, 1-2/3-4: T2-T3/T2-T3, rec. 10" **Cool down** • 400m easy **Total: 3100m**		
Sunday			50' AET1
TOTAL	6000m	192 min	120 min
TOTAL	**7h 10 min**		

Day	Swimming	Cycling	Running
Monday		**Spec. strength on rollers** • 15' easy • 5x3' high resistance, 40-60 rpm, rec. 3' easy • 15' easy Total: 57'	
Tuesday			45' AET1
Wednesday	**Warm up** • 100 relax • 25 la/25 ra/25 catch-up / 25 ticking armpit • 50 relax • 4x25 climax, V.1' • 100 relax **Core** • 3x800 1) relax, p.+p.b., 1/3 2) T2 1/3 3) 4x200 T3, rec. 15" • 100 relax **Cool down** • 300 relax **Total: 3100 meters**		
Thursday			30' AET2
Friday		**Spec. strength on rollers** • 15' easy • 5 x 3 high resistance, 40-60 rpm, rec. 3' easy • 15' easy Total: 57'	

Day	Swimming	Cycling	Running
Saturday	**Warm up** • 200m easy • 4x25m climax • 100m relax **Core** • 2400m locomotion **Cool down** • 400m easy **Total: 3200m**	120' LSD	
Sunday	60' AET1		
TOTAL	6300m	234 min	135 min
TOTAL	**8h 15 min**		

Day	Swimming	Cycling	Running
Monday		**Spec. strength on rollers** • 15' easy • 6x3' high resistance, 40-60 rpm, rec. 3' easy • 15' easy **Total: 63'**	
Tuesday			45' AET1
Wednesday	**Warm up** • 100 relax 1/3 • 200 techn. **Core** • 800, easy, register intermediate time 600 • 600, quicker than intermediate time above, register intermediate time 400 • 400, quicker than intermediate time above, register intermediate time 200 • 200, quicker than intermediate time above • 100 relax • 4x25 climax, V.1' **Cool down** • 400 relax **Total: 2900 meters**		
Thursday			30' AET2
Friday		**Spec. strength on rollers** • 15' easy • 6x3' high resistance, 40-60 rpm, rec. 3' easy • 15' easy **Total: 63'**	

Day	Swimming	Cycling	Running
Saturday	**Warm up** • 200m easy • 4x25m climax • 100m relax **Core** • 600m T2, rec. 1' • 3x200m, 1-3: T1-T3, rec. 30" • 6x100m, T3, rec. 15" • 12x50m, T3, rec. 10' **Cool down** • 400m easy **Total: 3300m**	150' LSD	
Sunday			75' AET1
TOTAL	6200m	282 min	150 min
TOTAL	**9h 15 min**		

Week 8: recovery

Day	Swimming	Cycling	Running
Monday			
Tuesday			
Wednesday		60 min on rollers	
Thursday			50' AET2
Friday		Spec. strength on rollers • 15' easy • 6 x 3 high resistance, 40-60 rpm, rec. 3' easy • 15' easy Total: 63'	
Saturday	Warm up • 3x (75mrelax-25mclimax) • 4x50m techn. Core • 10x100m, alt. T1-T2, rec. 15" • 100m relax • 10x100m, alt. T1-T3, rec. 15" • 100m relax Cool down • 400m easy Total: 3100 meters		60' AET1
Sunday		120' LSD	
TOTAL	3100	246 min	110 min
TOTAL	7h 10 min		

Week 9

Day	Swimming	Cycling	Running
Monday		**Spec. strength on rollers** • 15' easy • 7 x 3 high resistance, 40-60 rpm, rec. 3' easy • 15' easy **Total: 69'**	
Tuesday			45' AET1
Wednesday	**Warm up** • 200m relax • 4x50m techn. • 100m relax **Core** • 2x1000m 1) progr. each 250m (each 250m slightly faster) 2) 4x (200m relax – 50m slightly higher tempo) **Cool down** • 400m relax **Total: 2900 meters**		
Thursday			35' AET2
Friday		**Spec. strength on rollers** • 15' easy • 7 x 3' high resistance, 40-60 rpm, rec. 3' easy • 15' easy **Total: 69'**	
Saturday	**Warm up** • 100m relax • 200m slightly progr. each 50 • 2x50m techn. Rec. 10" **Core** • 3x900m 1) T3 1/5 2) T4 1/3 3) 3x300m T4, rec. 15" **Cool down** • 400m relax. **Total: 3500 meters**	150' LSD	
Sunday	60' AET1		
TOTAL	6400m	288 min	140 min
TOTAL	**9h 20 min**		

Week 10

Day	Swimming	Cycling	Running
Monday		**Spec. strength on rollers** • 15' easy • 7x3 high resistance, 40-60 rpm, rec. 3' easy • 15' easy **Total: 69'**	
Tuesday			45' AET1
Wednesday	**Warm up** • 200m relax • 4x50m techn., rec. 15" • 100m relax • 3x (50m relax – 25m climax) **Core** • 5x400m, 1-3/4-5: T1-T3/T1-T3, rec.30" **Cool down** • 400m easy **Total: 3125m**		
Thursday			30' AET2
Friday			90' AET2
Saturday	**Warm up** • 100m relax • 4x50m techn. • 2x25m climax, V.1' • 2x (12.5m relax – 12.5m sprint), rec. 20" • 100 relax **Core** • 4x400m, 1-2/3-4: T2 – T4/ T3 – T4, rec. 30" • 100m relax • 4x100m, total time faster than 4x400m above, rec. 10" **Cool down** • 400m relax **Total: 3000 meters**	180' LSD	
Sunday			75' AET1
TOTAL	6300m	339 min	150 min
TOTAL	**10h 05 min**		

Week 11

Day	Swimming	Cycling	Running
Monday		**Spec. strength on rollers** • 15' easy • 8x3 high resistance, 40-60 rpm, rec. 3' easy • 15' easy **Total: 75'**	
Tuesday			60' AET1
Wednesday	**Warm up** • 400m relax 1/3 • 200m techn. **Core** • 1000m T1 • 800m, T2 • 600m, T3 • 4x25m climax, V.1' **Cool down** • 400m relax **Total: 3500 meters**		
Thursday			35' AET2
Friday		90' suppleness	
Saturday	**Warm up** • 100 relax • 4x50 techn., rec.10" • 4x (25relax-25climax), rec. 15" • 100 relax **Core** • 4x200 T3, rec. 10" • 100 relax • 4x200 T4, rec. 15" • 100 relax • 1x200 T5 **Cool down** • 400 relax **Total: 3000 meters**	210' LSD	
Sunday			80' AET1
TOTAL	6500m	375 min	175 min
TOTAL	**11h 20 min**		

Week 12: recovery

Day	Swimming	Cycling	Running
Monday			
Tuesday			
Wednesday		60 min rollers	
Thursday			50' AET2
Friday		120' easy	
Saturday	2000 easy with techn.		75' AET1
Sunday		120' LSD	
TOTAL	2000	300 min	125 min
TOTAL	**7h 45 min**		

Week 13

Day	Swimming	Cycling	Running
Monday		15' AET1 60' AET3 15' AET1	Transition 10' very easy
Tuesday			60' AET1
Wednesday	**Warm up** • 4x (75m easy – 25m climax) • 100m easy **Core** • 2x500m, 1-2: T1 – T3, rec.30" • 100m easy • 4x250m, 1-2: T2 – T3 • 100m easy • 4x25m climax, V.1' **Cool down** • 400m relax **Total: 3200 meters**		
Thursday			10' AET1 20' AET3 10' AET1
Friday		60' AET1	
Saturday	**Warm up** • 300m easy • 8x25m: 8 x (12.5m easy – 12.5m sprint), rec. 30" • 100m easy **Core** • 6x100m, T2, rec. 10" • 100 relax • 6x100m T3, rec. 15" • 100 relax • 6x100m T4, rec. 30" • 100m relax • 2x100m T5, rec. 30" **Cool down** • 400 relax **Total: 3300 meters**	60' AET1 60' AET2 60' AET1	
Sunday			90' AET1
TOTAL	6500m	330 min	200 min
TOTAL	**11h**		

Week 14

Day	Swimming	Cycling	Running
Monday		*Recovery day*	
Tuesday		90' AET2	Transition 30' AET1
Wednesday	**Warm up** • 4x (75m easy – 25m climax) • 100m easy **Core** • 1200m T1, rec. 1' • 800 T2, rec. 1' • 600 T3 **Cool down** • 400m relax **Total: 3500 meters**		
Thursday			10' AET1 20' AET3 10' AET1
Friday		60' AET1	
Saturday	**Warm up** • 300m easy • 8x25m techn. • 100m easy **Core** • 2x400m, 1-2: T2 – T3, rec.30" • 4x200m, 1-2/3-4: T1 – T3, T2 – T4, rec. 15" • 8x100m, alt. T2 – T4, rec. 10" **Cool down** • 400 relax **Total: 3400 meters**	60' AET1 120' AET2 60' AET1	
Sunday			90' AET1
TOTAL	6900m	390 min	200 min

TOTAL 12h 20 min

Week 15

Day	Swimming	Cycling	Running
Monday		*Recovery day*	
Tuesday		60' AET2	Transition 30' AET1
Wednesday	**Warm up** • 400m easy • 4x50m: 4 x (25m easy – 25m tempo) • 100m easy **Core** • 1200m T2 • 3x400m, 1-3: T2 – T3, rec.30" **Cool down** • 400m relax **Total: 3500 meters**		
Thursday			15' AET1 50' AET2 10' AET1 **Total: 75'**
Friday		60' AET1	
Saturday	**Warm up** • 300m easy • 3x75m: 1-3, rec.15" • 100m easy **Core** • 6x200m, alt. T1 – T4, rec. 15" • 100m easy • 12x100m, alt. T2 – T4, rec. 10" **Cool down** • 400 relax **Total: 3525 meters**	270' AET1	Transition 10' easy
Sunday			105' AET1
TOTAL	7025 m.	390 min	220 min
TOTAL	**12h 45 min**		

Week 16: recovery

Day	Swimming	Cycling	Running
Monday		*Recovery day*	
Tuesday		*Recovery day*	
Wednesday	2000m easy		
Thursday			45' AET2
Friday		60' AET1	
Saturday	**Warm up** • 400m easy **Core** • 2400m locomotion **Cool down** • 400m relax **Total: 2800 meters**	240' AET1	
Sunday			75' AET1
TOTAL	4800m	300 min	120 min
TOTAL	**8h 40 min**		

Week 17

Day	Swimming	Cycling	Running
Monday		60' AET1 30' AET2	Transition 10' very easy
Tuesday			60' AET1
Wednesday	**Warm up** • 4x (175m easy – 25m climax) **Core** • 4x600m, 1-2/3-4: T2-T3/ T1-T4, rec. 30" **Cool down** • 400m relax **Total: 3600 meters**		
Thursday			40' AET2
Friday		60' AET1	
Saturday	**Warm up** • 200m easy • 3x (50m relax – 25m climax) • 100m easy **Core** • 1500m easy, p. • 3x500m T4, rec.30" **Cool down** • 400 relax **Total: 3925 meters**	270' AET1 – AET2	
Sunday			75' AET1
TOTAL	7525m	420 min	175 min
TOTAL	**12h 25 min**		

Day	Swimming	Cycling	Running
Monday		*Recovery day*	
Tuesday		90' AET2	Transition 30' AET1

Wednesday	**Warm up**
	• 4x (50m easy – 25m climax – 15m easy – 10m sprint)
	Core
	• 3x800m
	  1) easy with p.
	  2) T2
	  3) 8 x 100m T3, rec. 10"
	• 100m easy
	• 4x25m climax, rec. 30"
	Cool down
	• 400m easy
	Total: 3400 meters		

Thursday			15' AET1 30' AET3 15' AET1
Friday		60' AET1	
Saturday	**Warm up** • 200 relax • 4x (25 relax – 25 climax legs) • 100 relax **Core** • 800 T3 1/5 • 100 relax • 2x400 T4, rec. 15" • 100 relax • 4x200 T4, rec. 15" **Cool down** • 400 relax **Total: 3500 meters**	300' AET1-AET2	
Sunday			120' AET1
TOTAL	6900m	450 min	210 min
TOTAL	**13h 30 min**		

Week 19

Day	Swimming	Cycling	Running
Monday		*Recovery day*	
Tuesday		150' AET2	
Wednesday	**Warm up** • 400m easy **Core** • 3000m cont. swimming, T2 **Cool down** • 400m relax Total: 3800 meters		
Thursday			15' AET1 50' AET2 15' AET1 **Total: 80**
Friday		60' AET1	
Saturday	**Warm up** • 300 relax • 4x25 climax, V.1' • 100 relax **Core** • 4x600: 1) 200 high tempo – 400 relax 2) 400 relax – 200 high tempo 3) 200 high tempo – 200 relax – 200 high tempo 4) T4 rec. each time 30" **Cool down** • 500 relax Total: 3400 meters	300' AET1	
Sunday			120' AET1
TOTAL	7200 m.	510 min	210 min
TOTAL	**14h 30 min**		

Day	Swimming	Cycling	Running
Monday		*Recovery day*	
Tuesday		*Recovery day*	
Wednesday		2000m easy	
Thursday			60' AET2
Friday			90' AET1
Saturday	**Warm up** • 400m easy **Core** • 20x100m, alt. T1 – T3 • 100m easy • 10x50m, alt. T1 – T3 **Cool down** • 400m relax **Total: 3400 meters**	240' AET1 – AET2	
Sunday			90' AET1 with tempo changes: 4x6' AET3
TOTAL	5400m	360 min	150 min

TOTAL	**10h 10 min**

Week 21

Day	Swimming	Cycling	Running
Monday		*Recovery day*	
Tuesday		30' AET2 30' AET3	Transition 10' AET 3 50' easy
Wednesday	**Warm up** • 400m techn • 2x (25m easy – 25m climax) • 100m easy **Core** • 4x (175m easy – 25m kick), rec.15" • 8x (75m easy – 25m climax), rec.10" • 8x (25m tempo – 75m easy), rec.10" **Cool down** • 400m relax **Total: 3400 meters**		
Thursday			60' AET2
Friday		60' AET1	
Saturday		270' AET1 – AET2	Transition 45' AET1
Sunday	**Warm up** • 200m easy • 300m techn. **Core** • 2x300m, 1-2: T1 – T2, rec.30" • 100m easy • 3x250m, 1-3: T1 – T3, rec.30" • 100m easy • 4x150m, 1-2/3-4: T1-T3/T2-T4, rec.30" • 100m easy • 5x100m, T4, rec.15" **Cool down** • 400 relax **Total: 3550 meters**	75' AET1	
TOTAL	6990m	390 min	195 min
TOTAL	**12h 05 min**		

Day	Swimming	Cycling	Running
Monday		*Recovery day*	
Tuesday		90' AET2	Transition 30' AET2 10' AET1
Wednesday	**Warm up** • 200m easy **Core** • 3x1000m, 1-3, T1 – T3, rec. 1' • 4x200m, alt. T1 – T3, rec.10" **Cool down** • 400m relax **Total: 4400 meters**		
Thursday			15' AET1 3x12' AET3, rec.5' easy 15' AET1
Friday		60' AET1	
Saturday	**Warm up** • 200 relax • 200m techn. • 100 relax **Core** • 2400m locomotion **Cool down** • 400 relax **Total: 3300 meters**	300' AET1-AET2	
Sunday	120' AET1		
TOTAL	7700m	450 min	236 min
TOTAL	**14h 10 min**		

Week 23

Day	Swimming	Cycling	Running
Monday		*Recovery day*	
Tuesday		120' easy	
Wednesday	**Warm up** • 4x (75m easy – 25m climax) **Core** • 3800m cont. swimming, T2 **Cool down** • 200m easy **Total:4400 meters**		
Thursday		60' AET 1	
Friday		60' AET1	
Saturday		300' AET1	
Sunday	2000m easy, techn.		90' AET1
TOTAL	6400m	480 min	150 min

TOTAL	**12h 45 min**

Week 24: race week

Day	Swimming	Cycling	Running
Monday		*Recovery day*	
Tuesday		120' easy	
Wednesday			45' AET1
Thursday		90' AET1	
Friday		*Recovery day*	
Saturday	1500m easy		
Sunday	3800m	180km	42 km

Overview

Week	Swimming (meter)	Cycling (min)	Running (min)	Total
1	4800	150	120	6h 10 min
2	5050	180	120	6h 45 min
3	5600	204	145	7h 50 min
4	2300	184	100	5h 30 min
5	6000	192	120	7h 10 min
6	6300	234	135	8h 15 min
7	6200	282	150	9h 15 min
8	3100	246	110	7h 10 min
9	6400	288	140	9h 20 min
10	6300	339	150	10h 05 min
11	6500	375	175	11h 20 min
12	2000	300	125	7h 45 min
13	6500	330	200	11h
14	6900	390	200	12h 20 min
15	7025	390	220	12h 45 min
16	4800	300	120	8h 40 min
17	7525	420	175	12h 25 min
18	6900	450	210	13h 30 min
19	7200	510	210	14h 30 min
20	5400	360	150	10h 10 min
21	6990	390	195	12h 05 min
22	7700	450	236	14h 10 min
23	6400	480	150	12h 45 min
24	race week			

CHAPTER 9

Improving Your Performance by Correct Nutrition

Two of the most important performance determining factors, besides your actual training, are your nutrition pattern and your fluid intake.

To improve your insight into the importance of a good nutrition pattern, we should consider the energy supplies of the body.

The two largest energy sources of the body are carbohydrates and fatty acids. In extreme circumstances protein can also be an energy source. In this last case, however, the muscles are literally demolished, which would obviously lead to a loss of condition within a very short period.

When are fatty acids and carbohydrates used as an energy sources?

During very low intensity efforts, fatty acids are almost exclusively used as your energy source. If the effort intensity increases, the share of carbohydrates will increase as an energy supplier, and during very intensive efforts, energy is exclusively provided by oxidation of carbohydrates. These carbohydrates have been piled up in the body under the form of glycogen in the muscles and in the liver. But this carbohydrate stock is limited. Generally it is believed that during very intense efforts the carbohydrate stock is consumed after approximately 90 minutes.

Research has shown that on average, after intensive training sessions, only 5% of the muscle glycogen consumed while training is replaced per hour. When muscle glycogen is completely exhausted, it takes up to 20 hours before the muscle glycogen stocks again reach a normal level.

The fat stock in the body, on the other hand, is seemingly inexhaustible. The disadvantage of drawing upon energy supplied by oxidation of fatty acids in comparison with the oxidation of carbohydrates is that the fatty acid supply gets started more slowly, and less energy is provided than by oxidation of carbohydrates, for the same quantity of oxygen taken in.

Guidelines during and after training sessions with low intensity

When you train at low intensity during a very long and easy bike training, fatty acids are consumed as an energy source. Especially when preparing for long distances you will do a lot of training sessions at relatively low intensity. For all bike training sessions over 3 hours, you should use solid food that is lightly digestible. Energy-bars are very suitable to serve this purpose.

Since there is a sufficiently large stock of this energy source in the body, after the training sessions you can maintain a normal nutrition pattern, which consists on average of 60% carbohydrates, 25% fatty acids and 15% protein.

Supplementing fluid loss

For long training sessions (more than 1 hour) it is essential that fluid loss is always sufficiently compensated, during and also after training. This loss of fluids (perspiration) has to do with the regulation of the body temperature. The vaporization of the sweat ensures the cooling of the body. This sweat vaporization rate is strongly influenced by temperature and humidity.

The body temperature rises much more rapidly in warm than in cool weather. Sweat evaporates quicker in warm and dry weather and will cool the body more rapidly than in warm and wet weather. This is particularly important for long-term efforts.

Abundant perspiration may have an damaging impact on the body. Research has shown that a loss of only 1% already leads to performance loss. A 3% to 5% loss can reduce your performance capacity by as much as 10% to 30%.

Why is that the case?

By reduction of blood volume, blood becomes less liquid. Because of this, the heart will pump less effectively. Less oxygen can be transported to the working muscles and less sweat will be produced.

There will therefore be less sweat vaporization, which will lead to the body temperature increasing. Thus for endurance sportsmen like triathletes, the rectal temperature can rise in extreme cases to 40°C/104°F and higher. A temperature of 41°C/106°F is very dangerous and can cause irreparable damage to the liver, kidneys and brain.

Overheating can lead to the heat cramps, heat exhaustion and eventually heat collapse.

Heat cramps generally occur in the calves when a person sweats heavily without compensating for the fluid loss. Heat exhaustion soon follows, and when it does, activities must be immediately stopped.

Heat collapse is the most critical form of overheating, and is not always preceded by cramps or exhaustion. Heat collapse blocks the thermoregulating mechanisms, and as a result, body temperature will increase drastically. Immediate admission to a hospital is vital, and aid must ensure a fast cooling by water, ice or air.

It is wrong to think that overheating can only occur in endurance races in warm and wet weather. Long and difficult efforts in moderate conditions can also increase body temperature drastically.

You must therefore, for long-term efforts in all weather conditions, keep paying attention to cooling and supplementing your fluid stocks!

Completing your fluid stock is best done by means of water or the so-called thirst quencher. A thirst quencher consists of water, a restricted quantity of carbohydrates and also minerals which compensate for those lost by sweating.

Research has shown that a good general condition gives the body a better resistance against heat. If you are well trained, you will be better resistant against warm and wet conditions.

Tips for training sessions and races in warm conditions

- If possible you must acclimatize, which means you must force up training during five to eight days progressively in the same temperature in which the race will take place.

- Cool down your body by sprinkling it with water.

- Do your races and training sessions dressed lightly.

- Drink sufficiently during the race or training session. This means approximately 10 to 15 cl of fresh beverages each 15 min. Drinking more does not make much sense, because your body can only take in approximately 75 cl fluid per hour.

Guidelines for training sessions with moderate intensity

Although the intensity is already a little bit higher during these training sessions, fatty acids are still used as the primary energy source. Depending on the training intensity, however, the share of carbohydrates used always increases. Replenishing the fluid lost by means of thirst quenchers is advisable here in order to compensate for the lost minerals and to supplement the glycogen reserves. Otherwise, normal, healthy nutrition should be sufficient.

Guidelines for training sessions with high intensity

If you train at high intensity, say, a threshold training session, carbohydrates are the primary source of energy.

It is best to have already replenished carbohydrates burned during training sessions lasting longer than one hour, in order to avoid an encounter with "the wall" or "the man with the hammer." The so-called **energy drinks** are very important here, because they allow you to replenish carbohydrates burned easily during training or races. Of course you still need to use thirst quenchers to compensate the fluid loss.

Guidelines after an intensive training session

After an intensive training session or after a race, supplementing the carbohydrate stock is very important. You should start with this supplement within 30 minutes after training. Recent research has shown that maximal recovery can be reached by a combination of carbohydrates and protein, in a proportion of 50%-50%. Most recovery drinks meet these conditions.

Protein ensures that the negative nitrogen balance resulting from the intensive effort is neutralized. Preferably the first intake is liquid (recovery drink). Later you can switch to solid food, such as rice, pasta, bread etc. The share of the carbohydrates in solid nutrition can be now forced up to 70%.

Food having a high share of carbohydrates has a double function. First, it leads to an increase in blood glucose so the exhausted muscles can be replenished.

Second, the body reacts to this increase in blood glucose with an insulin response to again regulate blood glucose. This insulin response is anabolic (muscle developing) because insulin stimulates the shaping of muscle protein.

Practically this means that you must start within 15 to 30 minutes after intensive training with the intake of 100g carbohydrates in combination with protein, followed by 100g carbohydrates every 2 hours following. It is advisable at the first and the second intake to use liquid carbohydrates (recovery drinks) because these are processed more rapidly than carbohydrates in solid form. Afterwards you can switch to food.

You can obtain 100 g carbohydrates from, for instance: 150 g muesli, 150 g raisins, 140 g spaghetti (raw), 350 g cooked rice, 500 g potatoes (cooked), 5 bananas, 200 g dried figs, 250 g whole-wheat bread.

Note

If carbohydrates must be taken in fast, you should choose products with a high glycemic index (GI). The GI is a measurement for the speed with which carbohydrates are incorporated into the blood and increase the blood sugar quality. Products having a high GI include white bread, whole-wheat bread, cornflakes, muesli, bananas and raisins. Pastas only have an average GI.

When you do not completely replace your carbohydrate stock after intensive training sessions and races, your recovery goes slower. After multiple days of intensive training you feel spiritless and your training output decreases. All this can have a very negative impact on your final performance capacity.

The nutrition before the race

Some days before the race

During the days preceding an important and tough triathlon, the energy supply (carbohydrate stock) in the body can be intensified by adapting both nutrition and training. This can allow fatigue to be postponed during the race.

Practically speaking, you should do as follows:

- Train intensively up to 5 to 6 days before the race
- Gradually reduce the training quantity and quality (tapering)
- Eat meals with a high share of carbohydrates during the last 3 days before the race

The day of the race

It is advisable to have a meal with a high share of carbohydrates (150-200 g carbohydrates) 6 to 3 hours before the race. This way the food has been digested at the start of the race.

Afterwards it is better not to eat carbohydrates anymore, because too many carbohydrates in the blood could bring about an insulin reaction. Insulin is the hormone that keeps your carbohydrate stock in your blood at the right level. Due to this insulin reaction, your sugar level may drop so much that you could feel tired and washed-out.

Carbohydrate intake just before the start of the race (5 to 10 minutes) causes no problem because these carbohydrates are only incorporated once the race has already started. During intense efforts there is no insulin reaction.

In warm and wet circumstances it can also be useful to build a fluid reserve. You can do this by drinking approximately 500ml water or thirst quencher during the last half hour before the race.

The nutrition during the race

In long distance races, energy is provided by the oxidation of fatty acids and carbohydrates. Fatty acids do not have to be built up, because the stock in the body is more than enough.

During the swim, you burn part of your carbohydrate stock, and therefore it is very important to replenish this stock as soon as possible, starting at the beginning of the bike.

During the first half of the bike you can do this by eating solid food, such as sandwiches and energy bars. What you eat must be precisely tested during your long bike training sessions to be sure it agrees with your system! You would best advised to test lightly digestible products with a high caloric value.

During cycling you must also drink a lot. Per hour you should take in at least 0.5 to 0.75 liters (in warm weather). During the cycling component of an Ironman distance race, this amounts to a total of 4 liters! More is useless, because your body cannot process a larger quantity. Vary water and energy drinks. For the change in taste, you could compose a drink yourself. There are triathletes who mix Coca Cola with water (proportion 1-1). Make sure that the carbonation (gas) has disappeared from the Coke by preparing the drink the day before. Shake the mixture   thoroughly, then leave the bottles open overnight!

Guidelines for healthy nutrition

As mentioned before, the nutrition of a triathlete must comprise 60% carbohydrates (during intensive training days and stage races even up to 70%), 20-25% fats and 15% protein.

Generally speaking, the following foods are advisable: lots of vegetables, preferably uncooked; a lot of fruit; pasta, rice, potatoes, brown bread; chicken and fish; skimmed and semi-skimmed dairy products; muesli and other cereals.

The following products are not recommended: fat meat products; fried food; whole dairy products; salt; excessive sweets (cakes, cookies, chocolate...); alcohol; crisps; ....

Furthermore, you must pay close attention to the fluid intake during the day. This means that during the day you must regularly drink water, even apart from training. Water is preferred to coffee, because coffee blocks the intake of Vitamin C, and has a water secreting impact, promoting dehydration.

TIP:
Particularly at breakfast, take sufficient Kcal to provide the energy for the training labor coming. It is also best to eat some snacks periodically to prevent feeling hungry. At night it is best to simply eat less.

Must fats be absolutely avoided?

Your nutrition is built around the intake of carbohydrates. This does not mean, however, that fats must be avoided systematically. On the contrary, if you train intensely and regularly, you should not be afraid to consciously eat fats as part of your regular diet.

Fats ensure, by means of LDL-cholesterol, the production of steroids, including the anabolic hormone testosterone. A light body weight and little body fat are connected in several studies with men having a very low testosterone level. This results in a slower recovery from training labor.

Although saturated fats cannot be avoided completely, unsaturated fats must be preferred. These are among other things found in vegetable oil, nuts, seeds and fat fish.

Do protein supplements have to be taken?

In contrast to the intake of carbohydrates, you can assume that a normal nutrition pattern always contains sufficient protein.

An endurance athlete has a daily protein need of approximately 1.3 g/ kilogram. An athlete weighing 70 kilograms needs approximately 91 g of protein per day. If you know that a piece of chicken weighing approximately 200 g already provides almost half of the daily amount, it should be clear that you do not have to supplement for extra protein. Besides the necessary protein intake (combined with carbohydrates) right after an intense training session or race, slight supplementing should be considered only at the beginning of a new training set-up.

Protein is the building material of the body. Protein is called up as an energy source only in extreme cases, i.e. at complete exhaustion of the glycogen stocks.

Share of Kcal, protein, fats and carbohydrates of some common nutrients by 100 g

	Kcal	Protein	Fat	Carbohydrates
Banana	88	1	0	20
Apple	50	0	0	12
Orange	47	1	0	11
Kiwi	40	1	0	9
Muesli without sugar	390	11	8	68
Muesli with sugar	396	11	11	64
Oat malt	363	13	7	62
Cornflakes	370	7	1	84
Muesli bar	440	5	17	67
Milk skimmed	37	4	0.1	5
Milk semi-skimmed	46	4	1.5	5
Milk whole	63	4	3.4	5
Yogurt skimmed	35	4	0.1	4
Yogurt semi-skimmed	49	4	1.5	5
Yogurt whole	85	5	4.5	6
Brown bread	248	10	3	45
Whole-wheat bread	222	9	3	41
Margarine	730	0	80	1
Cheese 20+	245	34	12	0
Cheese 50+	370	23	31	0
Ham, raw	199	23	12	0
Chicken roll	166	24	7	2
Chocolate sprinklings	431	6	17	64
Marmalade	112	0	0	28

	Kcal	Protein	Fat	Carbohydrates
Spaghetti raw	350	12	2	71
Spaghetti cooked	94	3	1	19
Pizza, cheese and tomato	211	10	10	26
Rice unboiled	346	7	1	78
Rice cooked	147	3	0	33
Potato, cooked	76	2	0	17
Fries	310	5	15	38
Cauliflower, raw	14	2	0	2
Carrots, raw	11	1	0	2
Endive, raw	5	1	0	0
Peas, cooked	60	4	0	11
Raw vegetables	14	1	0	2
Tomatoes	11	1	0	2
Leek, raw	24	1	0	0
Vegetable soup	34	1	2	3
Cod fish, cooked	105	23	1	0
Salmon	271	28	18	0
Chicken filet	158	31	4	0
Turkey filet	158	31	4	0
Breakfast bacon	404	15	38	0
Pork tenderloin	147	28	4	0
Beefsteak	139	27	3	1
Roast beef	167	28	6	1
Pudding, vanilla	114	4	3	19
Ice cream	182	3	9	22

How about nutritional supplements and other preparations?

Concerning nutrition supplements and preparations, it is still difficult to see the forest for the trees.

Some supplements are actually supportive of your training labor:

- **Arginine and ornitine**
  Amino acids, which when administered in sufficiently large quantities stimulate the pituitary gland. Because of this, the production of the body-growing hormone is stimulated. This growing hormone improves recovery after effort.

- **Glutamine**
  An amino acid which reduces muscle demolition and reinforces the immune system.

- **Antioxidants**
  In the body, as a result of your metabolism and energy production, free radicals are being produced. These free radicals are, among other things, responsible for cardiac diseases, some forms of cancer, aging and muscular ache after effort. Research has also shown that training increases the amount of free radicals.

  Antioxidants are substances that neutralize the damaging functions of free radicals. Thus the damage to muscle cells would be reduced for athletes who take supplemental antioxidants than for those who do not take these supplements.

- **Vitamins and mineral supplements**
  Quite a lot of athletes take such supplements, often in very large quantities. These supplements are necessary when you do not eat enough fruit and vegetables. A triathlete who eats 4 to 6 pieces of fruit every day and plenty of fresh vegetables does not need these expensive preparations.

- **Vitamin C**
  This vitamin nevertheless deserves particular attention. On the one hand it belongs to the antioxidants group, but on the other hand it has been proven that vitamin C raises the resistance of the body against infections.

  A triathlete who trains intensely has an lower resistance to infections, because the strain has decreased that resistance. Vitamin C raises this resistance back to a sufficiently high level. One to two grams/day during periods of intense training and races seems suitable. When infections arise, some doctors even prescribe five grams/day.

- **Iron**
  Iron supplements are only significant if there is an iron shortage, i.e. too low ferritine levels. Many athletes systematically take iron preparations, even without a documented shortage. This makes no sense, since and iron surplus, resulting in in the spinal cord and organs such as the liver can be dangerous.

General conclusion

1. Always drink sufficiently, even in cooler weather. Also drink during training sessions if possible, but if not, certainly immediately after.

2. Replenish the energy stocks during intensive training sessions and races, preferably by means of energy drinks. Per hour, 60-70 g carbohydrates must be consumed.

3. Always replenish energy stocks after intensive training sessions and races. Within 15 to 30 minutes after the training session/race, start using recovery drinks with a proportion of 50% carbohydrates and 50% protein.

4. After using the energy drinks, the muscles must be reactivated with meals having a high share of carbohydrates (bread, rice, pasta, potatoes).

5. Adjust the nutrition pattern as a function of training labor. The energy intake during recovery days must be significantly lower than during intensive training days or race days.

6. Nutrition products with a high share of carbohydrates must be the main part of your nutrition program.

7. Make sure that fat still accounts for 20% of the total nutrition pattern. It is wrong to systematically ban it from your nutrition.

8. Consciously limit the weight increase during the relative rest period.

9. When overweight, scale back your body weight to your ideal weight gradually

10. Never economize on the intake of carbohydrates during a diet.

CHAPTER 10

Overtraining and Tips to Prevent Overtraining

What is overtraining?

Triathlon is a passion, and is literally addictive. Quite soon you will compare distances and times, with yourself, and with others. How long? How far? Quicker and further. You always want more.

You may feel that you trained well and extensively, but suddenly your results stagnate and later slacken. Often this prompts you to train even harder, devouring still more kilometers without any improvement. On the contrary, performances will often decline even further. How is that possible?

To answer this question we need to analyze the term training.

Training is administering systematic physical stimulations to the body, taking into account the capacity of the body. These stimulations bring about changes in the body which lead, when considering the correct proportion of effort and recovery, to an increase of the performance capacity.

In this definition there are some important data:
- Taking into account the capacity of the body

Triathlon is indeed a very straining sport, and every triathlete has a certain training capacity. This capacity can vary from one day to the next. Insufficient sleep, bad nutrition, illness, or stress can all reduce the capacity of the body.

Not every triathlete has the same capacity. Some triathletes can perform more training labor than others. Therefore it makes no sense to just copy training set-ups of other successful triathletes.

It is far more important to take into account the training principles applied by good triathletes, and apply these principles while considering your own capacity. It is not so that the triathlete with the largest capacity by definition also obtains the best results. Some athletes can achieve better results with less training than athletes who train harder and more frequently.

Overtraining arises if the training stimuli are stronger than the individual's capacity. It is possible to distinguish **qualitative overtraining** and **quantitative overtraining**.

The cause for **qualitative overtraining** is typically found in the intensity of the training pivots, i.e. you train too intensively. In **quantitative overtraining,** on the other hand, the training volume is too large – the training duration is too long. Overtraining often appears as a combination of these two forms.

Therefore it is very important that training intensity and training volume are forced up gradually. In the beginning of a training set-up you should first pay attention to gradually forcing up training volume. In other words, you must always strive for extensive basic endurance (aerobic endurance) before starting to train more intensively.

You constantly have to give your body the opportunity to adapt to a rising training workload. Intensifying the training workload too suddenly, qualitatively or quantitatively, leads to a drop in performance level after a while.

At that moment you are very susceptible to overload injuries. Especially when starting a new training program, after some time off or after a tough race period, you should handle your training with care. Even for the best-trained triathletes, there is a shaky balance between performance improvement and overtraining.

- Consider the correct proportion of effort – recovery:
It may sound strange, but training itself decreases performance levels. By the end of the training session you are tired and not able to repeat the session. A positive training impact is possible only after a sufficiently long recovery period. This mechanism is called the **principle of supercompensation.**

The principle of supercompensation

The principle of supercompensation is the most important training principle for a triathlete, but at the same time it also is the most difficult to apply.

According to this principle, the training impact can only be obtained when training is followed by a sufficiently long recovery period.

This seems very logical, but for a triathlete who has to train for three different disciplines, the application of this principle is far from simple.

Next diagram explains this principle:

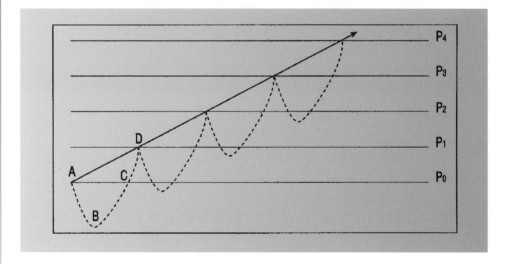

Po, P1, P2, P3, P4: Different performance levels
AB: Drop in the performance level as a result of training fatigue
BC: Rise in the performance level during recovery period
CD: The supercompensation. As a result of the training labor, the
   performance level of the athlete rose to a higher level.

We see that optimum training impact can only be obtained if the next training stimulation happens after the top of supercompensation (D) has been reached.

As a triathlete you are faced with a number of fundamental questions:
- When have you fully recovered to start training again (in other words how much time do you need to reach supercompensation after a certain training session)?
- How intense can this next training session be?
- What is the influence of training for other disciplines on the time needed to reach supercompensation after a training session?

The time to reach supercompensation is determined by a number of elements

- *Your degree of training*
  You will recover sooner if you are well trained.

- *The nature of the training session*
  The more intense the training session is, the longer the recovery phase lasts. Slow endurance bike training demands significantly less recovery time than intensive interval run training.

- *Training sessions done during the recovery phase of your training*
  An endurance training session for swimming is less straining after an intensive bike training session than a long endurance run.

- *Correct nutrition*
  Being a triathlete, you demand a lot from your body. You train several hours a day, which consumes a lot of energy. The correct nutrition in combination with thirst quenchers, energy and recovery drinks (see elsewhere) is essential for an optimal recovery phase.

- *Your mental state*
  There is a clear link between your mental state and your recovery time after training. If you are mentally stressed for whatever reason, you will recuperate slower (thus you need more time to reach supercompensation) in comparison to being relaxed.

- *A normal sleep pattern*
  A normal sleep pattern is also important. Because of a series of hormonal processes, it is important to go to bed early and to get

up early. The testosterone quality in blood undergoes an increase during the night to reach a peak in the morning.

The human growth hormone, which among other things is responsible for the recovery of the body after intense efforts, reaches maximum values during the night.

A good night's rest optimizes the functioning of these hormones.

- **Blood analysis on a regular basis**
  Due to frequent and demanding training sessions, it is possible that certain shortages arise in the blood. Regular blood analysis can help discover possible shortages (e.g. Fe, B12 etc.) so you can address them immediately.

Indications in order to determine the top of supercompensation

- **Your subjective feeling**
  If you feel tired, you will certainly not yet have reached the top of supercompensation. There is, of course, "normal" fatigue" after a rough training session. Sometimes fatigue lingers, even after a normal night's rest, and your legs feel sluggish and even painful while training.

  Continuing to complete your training does not make sense. You must always keep in mind that a tired body is not trainable; on the contrary you can only reverse the training effect by training more. Triathletes are very passionate, and therefore it is often hard to admit you feel tired.

- **Blood analyses**
  By means of a series of parameters, such as the number of red blood cells, hemoglobin quality, the haematocrite value (the proportion of the number of red blood cells to the total plasma volume) etc., doctors can establish whether or not you are wearing yourself out by training. Such analyses are however rather expensive and can only be carried out a few times per year.

- *Submaximal or maximal tests*
  The performance level during these tests, paired with other parameters such as the curve of the heart rate during the test, can offer an idea of the recovery process.

- *The registration of the heart rate during training*
  If you are used to training and using a heart rate monitor you can observe quite quickly whether your training heart rate is "normal" based on the effort made.

  If you realize that your heart rate is higher than usual, this can be an indication that you have not yet recuperated sufficiently from the preceding training session. It is also possible that a low heart rate, or the feeling that you cannot increase the heart rate, indicates fatigue (see further).

- *A clear insight in the type of the training sessions undertaken*
  It is advisable to keep a training diary. When you are well aware of the type of training you have done, you can adjust, in case of fatigue, your recovery phase.
  The next table shows the recovery time needed in function of the nature of the training session.

Recovery time after different types of training intensity

Recovery time ↓	Type of work load →	Aerobic	85-95% Aerobic/ anaerobic	95-100% Anaerobic	Strength
During the effort		Intensity 60-70%			
Immediate but incomplete recovery			After 1.5 to 2 h	After 2 h	After 2 h
90-95% recovery		At intensity 75-80% after 12 h	After 12 h to 18 h	After 12	After 18 h
Complete recovery		At intensity 75-80% after 24 to 36 h	After 24 to 48 h	After 48 to 72 h	After 72 to 84 h

From this table you can deduce, among other things, that you have to wait at least 3 days after an intensive training session before you may do the same session again.

All this does not mean that you cannot train during the recovery phase after intensive training. After a very intensive training session (with repeated efforts on an anaerobic level), recovery training is, in the first place, advisable. After a more moderate intensive session (training sessions around threshold), easy long endurance training of another discipline can be undertaken without any problems occurring. This training session must then again be followed by recovery training.

- *The recording of resting heart rate (see p. 36)*

(see p. 36)

All the previous data shows that your training labor is only effective if sufficient (relative) recovery time is inserted after training to reach supercompensation.

What happens if the recovery time after training has not been sufficient becomes clear from the next diagram:

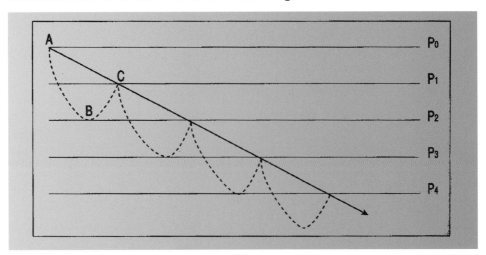

Po, P1, P2, P3, P4: Different performance levels
AB: Drop in the performance level as a result of training fatigue.
BC: The rise in the performance level during the recovery period is insufficient due to insufficient recovery time. A new training stimulus was inserted too early. As a result of this there is no supercompensation and we see a drop, instead of a rise, of the performance level.

Other causes of overtraining

You must learn to listen to your body. Painful and rigid muscles, a general feeling of fatigue, a stagnation or fall of the performance level, or a raised resting heart rate often are indications that the training intensity (quantitatively and/or qualitatively) is too high. Drastically diminishing the training quantity or even complete rest is recommended to avoid a situation that is getting worse and worse.

It is not always easy to even scale back training. You are soon afraid that months of training labor is lost if you reduce or stop training for a few days.

The causes of overtraining are often situated outside training

- *Successive races without sufficient chance for recovery*

- *Stress, mental difficulties*
  Relationship problems, etc. reduce the individual capacity. In a training plan you need to take into account "difficult periods", during which you cannot train as much.

- *Insufficient sleep*
  It is vitally important to sleep sufficiently. A good night's rest is essential, and even a short nap after a straining training session can have a positive effect.

- *Infection, such as influenza*
  Just like when the body is fatigued, an important principle should be applied here: a sick body is never, under absolutely any circumstances, trainable. It is often difficult to interrupt training. You are afraid that training labor will be lost. But it does not make any

sense to train when sick, and is even dangerous. Absolute rest accelerates the healing process. Training when ill can leave long-term effects. Unfortunately some people still try to "sweat out" influenza. This idea is not only absurd, but it can be life-threatening.

- *Unbalanced diet*
  The nutrition pattern of a triathlete who trains several hours daily must be well conceived in light of these efforts. The share of carbohydrates in nutrition is especially important.

- *A negative energy balance*
  This means that more energy is consumed than taken in. This often occurs when striving for an unrealistic ideal weight by following a low-carb diet.

- *Dehydration*
  The fluid lost by perspiration must be replenished both during and after training. The idea of dressing "thick" during training, and reaching your ideal weight by means of perspiration, has very disadvantageous consequences on the performance level.

- *Heat*
  Warm and wet weather conditions decrease your capacity and performance potential. It is thus advisable to reduce the training workload in abnormally warm weather conditions.

- *Using medication*
  If you take medicines, you must always consult your doctor to know what impact these medicines will have on your capacity, and whether or not they have a negative impact when practicing a sport intensely.

- *Jetlag*
  It is a general belief that the time needed to adapt to the time difference amounts to one day per time zone change. When traveling long distances and undergoing the accompanying time zone changes, it is advisable to train very calmly during the first days.

Recognizing overtraining

To avoid overtraining it is not only necessary to know the causes of overtraining, but also to have insight into the symptoms.

An important symptom of overtraining is a decrease in the maximum performance capacity. But there are still a lot of other indications. You'll also notice that your heart rate increases less rapidly than usual, and that you have to put in more effort than normal to increase your heart rate to a certain level. Often this is preceded by a period in which your resting heart rate also has increased. Recovery after effort is slowed down, although in some cases, in spite of overtraining, the heart rate rapidly drops after effort.

Furthermore there are still a number of mental indications of overtraining. You do not feel like training, you are irritable, you are not very hungry and you sleep poorly. In addition you have an increased risk of infection.

A specific example of the raised risk on infections is herpes. Herpes is a viral infection which often appears as cysts (also called fever blisters) on the lip or around the mouth. Once contaminated by it, the virus that causes herpes is always latently present in the body. During periods of reduced capacitance, for example when training too much, this infection breaks through.

You also notice that you are more susceptible to colds during periods of heavy training, or when you are in good shape. Colds are the consequence of contact with certain viruses. If the immune system against these viruses is weak, the odds of catching a cold increase. Research has proven that intensive training weakens the immune system. Hence athletes in top condition, after they have trained intensely, are more subject to these viruses.

Recognizing overtraining is often difficult, because a low heart rate during the effort and a fast recovery of the heart rate after the effort can be interpreted as positive training impact. Moreover, during a lactic acid test for possible overtraining, a reduced lactic acid quality during effort is established. This can also lead to misinterpretation.

To recognize overtraining, much attention must be paid to your mental state. Do you feel good, are you eager to train, do you have a normal sleeping pattern and a normal appetite, and do you process training smoothly? When you start to feel like you are in a training rut, it is advisable to stop training or scale back.

A lot of scientists are convinced that overtraining is largely a mental issue. For this reason variations in training, and disruptions in training to pursue other entertainment not involving your sport are necessary.

It is also important to examine whether your heart rate obtains normal values during training. The heart rate which does not increase easily during training and therefore remains abnormally low in spite of increasing strain is often a sign that you are tired. It is again best to plan a recovery period.

In spite of all the previous observations, you cannot lose sight of the fact that you can be tired during a training session and a race without this necessarily implying overtraining. Before you can obtain positive training impact, you should be tired. It is, however, important that you insert sufficient recovery after efforts in order to reach supercompensation.

You should also distinguish overload from overtraining: In case of overload, fatigue disappears after a few days and you also will perform better after some recovery days.

In the case of overtraining, fatigue keeps on bugging you, even after some recovery days. Your performance level remains reduced.

How can you prevent overtraining?

Determining overtraining is not simple, because at first sight you generally attribute a reduction of the performance level with too little training rather than too much training. Determining overtraining with certainty often happens late. The consequence is that you keep trying to catch up with the facts. It is also difficult to determine the cause of overtraining. For this reason there are a number of means to help you.

Keeping a training diary

In the training diary, the following issues are noted day after day: precise description of the kind of training done: duration, distance, intensity; How was training experienced (easy, tough...); How does recovery go?; Registration of the resting heart rate; Weight; Mental state; possibly other observations.

When there are symptoms of overtraining, you can consult the training diary and look for the beginning of the overtraining and possible causes.

Tips to prevent overtraining

- Insert a day of rest or a relative recovery day when feeling tired
- Always try to get a good night's rest
- Take into account reduced resistance of the body in periods of stress, abnormally tough weather conditions, etc.
- Always make sure there is sufficient carbohydrate intake during and after intensive training sessions and races
- Always make sure there is enough fluid intake during and after training sessions and races, even when it is not really wet and warm
- An intensive training day should always be followed by a day of training extensively or by a relative recovery day
- Keep a daily training diary
- Scale back the training sessions sufficiently when preparing an important race
- Pay attention to all possible symptoms of overtraining

Impact of detraining

Permanent training impact is only realized and preserved when training is sufficiently intensive and the training program shows systematic regularity.

As mentioned before, the most important effects of endurance training are:
- An increase of the maximal oxygen intake (VO_2max)
  Research has shown that moderate endurance training raises VO_2max by 10 to 20%, and thorough and long-term endurance training can lead to an increase of up to 25% of VO_2max.

- An increase of the stroke volume. This means that the quantity of blood which is expelled by each heart beat increases, allowing more oxygen per heart rate to be transported to the active muscles.

- An increase in the number or capillaries surrounding individual muscle fibers. Because of this, the delivery of oxygen and nutrients to the muscles and the removal or metabolic waste products rises. The increase of the number of capillaries can amount to 50% above the values of untrained people.

What happens if training is interrupted?
- If training is interrupted entirely, one notices a strong drop of VO_2max during the first month, followed by a further, but slower fall during the following two months. The level of the VO_2max nevertheless is still higher than the level of untrained people. A limited positive impact remains, even after 3 months of "detraining."

- The fall of the stroke volume follows the same curve.

- The increased capillary density, on the other hand, remains the same for well-trained endurance athletes even after 3 months of detraining. For less well trained athletes a substantial fall may be determined.

We notice that completely interrupting training has a strong opposite impact: in just a few weeks' time much of a laboriously built condition is lost. Your condition, for which you perhaps have worked for years, disappears much faster than it took to build it.

It is nevertheless the case that you need significantly less time to again reach a certain conditioning level than it took you to initially reach that level.

After 10 days of detraining, it will require more than 10 days to return to the initial trained level. It will take more like 30 days to get back to the level you had at the beginning of your detraining. Theoretically, it will take 40 days to return to your initial level of conditioning for every 20 days of detraining.

Studies have, however, proven that an endurance athlete can preserve his condition during 20 weeks when training labor is reduced by 40%, keeping the intensity relatively identical.

Therefore you should not be afraid to lose your condition if you train a little less.

CHAPTER 11

Blood Analysis

Your eventual performance level is not only determined by your training, but also by a number of other factors.

A very important factor is the medical support. By means of regular blood control it can be established whether a triathlete has certain shortages and if training possibly needs to be adjusted.

Some important blood parameters which directly or indirectly influence performance are:

- **The red blood cells (RBC)**
  The RBC transport oxygen in the body. A high number of RBC is therefore favorable for a triathlete. Experience teaches that after a period of tough training sessions or races, the number of RBC often decreases. After a recovery period, an increase should occur. A fall in number of RBC can be an indication to scale back the training volume.

- **Hemoglobin**
  Hemoglobin is a protein which links itself with oxygen. A high hemoglobin quality is therefore of interest to triathletes because the oxygen transport rises. This quality is also affected by overly tough training sessions.

- **The haematocrite**
  This is the proportion of the number of RBC with respect to the total blood volume. For this reason, high haematocrite value indicates a high oxygen transport capacity, which is also very interesting for a triathlete.

- **Creatine kinase (CK)**
  CK is an enzyme that indicates muscle reduction. Overly intensive training sessions or insufficient recovery between the training sessions and/or races lead to a high CK-value. High CK-value is an absolute indication to reduce the training intensity.

- **Urea**
  Urea is a substance released when proteins are demolished. A too high urea level in athletes can indicate that too little fluid is taken in during and after the training sessions.

- **Testosterone**
  Testosterone is an anabolic (constructive) hormone. A fall in testosterone levels can indicate that the body is no longer processing your training. Reducing the training strain, both quantitatively and qualitatively, is strongly advisable in this case.

- **Cortisol**
  Cortisol is a catabolic (demolishing) hormone. An increase in cortisol levels indicates that training is no longer processed well. The proportion of testosterone to cortisol is also important. Fall of testosterone level and simultaneous increase of the cortisol level is an indication that the cyclist is not recuperating sufficiently.

- **Vitamin B12 and folic acid**
  Vitamin B12 and folic acid are needed to build proteins and RBC.

- **Ferritine**
  Ferritine is a protein iron complex which determines the iron reserve in the body. Iron is needed for the production of RBC and hemoglobin. A shortage of iron decreases hemoglobin levels and the number of RBC.

- **Magnesium**
  Magnesium is an important factor in energy metabolism and influences the nerve muscle sensitivity. Shortage of magnesium manifests itself clinically by a disturbed nerve muscle function (among other things cramps) and muscle weakness.

CHAPTER 12

Overload Injuries and How to Avoid Them

Overload injuries are a very annoying, but an almost inescapable consequence of regular and advanced training. It is dreaming of utopia to think that overload injuries can be completely avoided.

Most of the injuries are caused by run training. Running is a very straining sport, much more so than cycling and swimming.

While running, your body, and your feet in particular, need to absorb a great deal of shock. On average the pressure on the foot with every running step amounts to approximately three to four times the body weight. That is the reason why triathletes who weigh more generally are more liable to injuries than lighter athletes.

As long as the strain and the resistance capacity of the movement system are in balance, there are no problems. Overload injuries arise when the training strain exceeds the capacity of the body.

Every triathlete has their own individual capacity. For inexperienced triathletes this capacity can be exceeded quickly. Much has to do with the familiarization of the body to the run training imposed.

But even very experienced triathletes have to deal with the risk of overload injuries as well. In principle you could claim that a running volume of more than 60 kilometers per week implies potential risk of injuries for every triathlete, even for the most trained one.

TIP:
Interrupt the training immediately in case of an injury. Continuing to train with pain generally results in a long-term convalescence period.

Causes of injuries

- **A wrong, too-quick training set-up**
  Your body needs time to adapt to an increasing strain. You must also take into account that the physiological adaptation of your body generally comes about more rapidly than the adaptation of your movement system. In other words, it is possible that a certain strain does not mean exaggerated strain for your heart, blood cycle and breathing system, but that your joints, tendons and muscles have not yet been sufficiently adapted to the training labor imposed.

- **A too-long, always increasing training strain without interruption by a rest period**
  One could more or less compare this situation to an elastic bandbeing stretched slowly further and further. This lasts till the elastic snaps.

- **A too-heavy, one-time strain**
  Generally an overload injury is the consequence of a long-term process, a repeated strain. An overload injury can, however, also arise immediately when suddenly exaggerated heavy effort is required, for example, when a marathon is being run without sufficient training background.

- **Deviations in putting your foot down**

- **Running on a hard surface**
  Too much running on a hard surface can cause a lot of misery to Achilles tendons, the shinbone and the knees. A soft surface softens the shock significantly.

- **Running with unsuitable shoes**

- **Cycling with high resistance**
  Triathletes who regularly push with too much resistance are risking an inflammation of the knee tendon. Training with high resistance cannot be exaggerated and always needs to be varied with suppleness training.

- **Cycling with a too high or a too low saddle**
  A saddle that is too low often leads to inflammation of the knee tendon. A saddle that is too high, on the other hand, can cause pain in the backside of the leg in the knee fold.

Common injuries

Overload injuries can differ greatly, and can arise in almost any spot in the movement system. In a lot of cases these injuries are inflammations of the tendons (tendinitis) in particular.

Inflammation is generally accompanied by the following symptoms: looking red, feels hot, swelling, pain (sensitive to pressure).

Tendinitis should first and foremost be treated using ice therapy. This means that you put ice on the spot which is inflamed. It often is advisable to massage the inflamed spot with a piece of ice, so the spot of the injury becomes cold through and through. This treatment is also called ice friction.

Generally you cannot do anything wrong when putting ice on an inflamed tendon. In a lot of cases it is the best way to control the possibility of tendinitis without having to interrupt training entirely. In this case, the ice needs to be applied immediately after a strongly reduced effort, best for about 10 minutes, and several additional times a day.

If the injury nevertheless gets worse, you should interrupt training completely and visit a sports doctor.

TIP:
Be careful that you do not "burn" the skin when applying ice friction due to the direct contact of the ice with the skin. That is why you would best apply a thin bandage around the ice.

Some common injuries for runners are tendinitis of the Achilles tendon, plantar fasciitis, periostitis and runner's knee.

Tendinitis of the Achilles tendon

The Achilles tendon is a very large, firm tendon which forms the connection between the calf muscles and the heel bone.

Generally this injury starts unsuspiciously, with a vaguely teasing feeling. In spite of this vague pain you can initially still keep on training. But here is where we meet the great risk. Often you still keep running until the pain forces you to stop training. In that case the tendon is most of the time swollen and sensitive to pressure.

Possible causes:
- Forcing up training too fast for too much training volume;
- Running uphill;
- Running on a hard surface;
- Overpronation and oversupination of the foot, as a result of which the heel bone is being strained much more;
- Running shoes with a bad heel which does not absorb shocks sufficiently;
- Too short and rigid calf muscles, putting too much tension on the Achilles tendon;
- Cycling in cold and wet weather conditions.

Possible solutions:
- First of all, it is required to stop training. Chronic tendinitis of the Achilles tendon is very difficult to treat, because the tendon is not well supplied with blood. Complete immobilization by means of a plaster cast is the only option;
- If the position of the feet is deviated, adapted soles can relieve the Achilles tendon;
- A light raising of the heel;
- Running shoes with adapted heel which absorb shocks better;
- Stretching exercises for the calf muscles;
- Running on a soft, but levelled surface;
- Avoid running uphill;
- Keep feet and Achilles tendons warm during cycling trainingbike training sessions in cold and wet conditions;
- Ice therapy.

Runner's knee

Runner's knee is a term which includes a number of common knee injuries. This high rate of injuries is not astonishing if you realize that the knee is a complicated joint through which two bones meet, namely the thigh bone and the shinbone. The calf bone is not a part of the knee joint. The knee joint further comprises the ligaments (6), the menisci (2) and the knee-cap (patella).

Factors which create a heavy strain on the knee are:
- long-term strain
- high running speed
- running on a hard surface
- a deviating foot position
- a deviating knee position
- cycling with high resistance

The most common running injuries to the knee are:

Chondromalicia of the knee-cap
Chondromalicia is wear to the cartilage at the back of the knee-cap. The pain localizes itself at the front of the knee, over the complete joint. Running uphill and sitting with bended knees will worsen the pain.

Possible causes are:
- An instability of the joint;
- A deviation of the feet. Both flat feet and hollow feet can cause the development of this injury.

Possible solutions are:
- First of all, resting, followed by a gradual forcing-up of the training volume. The training sessions must be shortened in any case.
- Making the quadriceps stronger (front thigh muscle). This give the knee more stability and there will be less wear of the cartilage.
- Checking if there is a deviated position of the feet. If the answer is yes, adapted soles can solve the problem since they correct the position during running.

Chondromalicia requires a swift diagnosis. Cartilage is a fabric that does not get well supplied with blood. That is why convalescence can be lengthy.

Inflammation of the iliotibial tractus

The iliotibial tractus is a tendon plate which runs along the outer part of the thigh and attaches it to the outer part of the lower leg. When bending the knee this plate goes alongside the outer part of the knee over the femoral condyl. This is a projection of the lower part of the thigh bone.

When being overloaded at the top of this projection, friction causes inflammation. The pain arises after running, and can become so dramatic that you must stop running.

Possible causes are:
- O-legs
- A difference in leg length
- Oversupination of the foot
- Shortened or rigid muscles especially on the outer part of the thigh
- Too much running at the same side of a sloping road
- Too-fast training set-up
- Too much fast run training sessions

Possibly solutions:
- Stretching the outer part of the thigh muscles regularly
- A good warm-up before every intensive run training session
- Running shoes which are adapted to the foot statistic
- A good training set-up, with attention to gradually forcing up both the training volume and the training intensity.
- Running on flat roads. If the road slants, you best vary the running direction regularly.
- Apply ice immediately after the effort.

Tendinitis of the patella tendon

The patella tendon (knee tendon) connects the knee-cap to the upper, front part of the shinbone. This knee tendon is the continuation of the four-headed thigh muscle (quadriceps femoris) that makes sure the knee can be stretched. Especially for jumping athletes, this tendon undergoes heavy pressure. That is why the injury in which the knee tendon is infected is also called a jumper's knee.

An infection of the patella tendon can, however, occur with runners and cyclists as well. Due to a long-term strain, the tendon gets irritated right below the joint. In serious cases the pain isn't just felt during running and cycling, but also when getting up in the morning.

Possible causes
- Running uphill too often
- Deviating position of the feet
- Too high and/or too rapid training set-up
- Too rigid and short hindmost thigh muscles (hamstrings)
- Too weak front thigh muscles, as a result of which the knee tendon is being strained too much
- Cycling with high resistance;
- Bike saddle that is too low.

Possible solutions
- Scaling back of the training strain or undergoing a period of complete rest;
- Running shoes which are adapted to the foot statistic;
- Avoid running uphill;
- Stretching of the hindmost thigh muscles;
- Very gradual and progressive reinforcement of the four-headed thigh muscle;
- In case of infection: ice therapy;
- Suppleness cycling;
- Adjust bike saddle.

Plantar fasciitis

Under the foot sole there is a thick membrane that goes from the heel to the ball of the foot. This membrane gives support to the lower part of the foot. When too much pressure is put on this membrane, an inflammation can occur. The symptoms sometimes are pain in the complete lower part of the foot, sometimes only in the heel.

Often the pain is bearable in the beginning. If training is not interrupted, and if the cause of infection has not been removed the pain gets worse even to the extent that it becomes impossible to run any further.

This inflammation can turn out to be a very annoying, long-term injury when you keep on running with it too long. Swiftly interrupting training is a must.

Possible causes
- Too rapid increase of the training strain;
- Running with insufficiently flexible soles;
- Overpronation of the feet;
- Flat feet.

Possible solutions
- Immediately interrupting training when in pain;
- Gradual training set-up;

- Correct and high quality shoe choice;
- Adapted shoes in function of deviation of the foot;
- Possible adaptation by wearing insoles.

Shin splints

Shin splints arise when the pressure on the membrane covering the shinbone increases dramatically due to overload in the bottom third. Small tears in the membrane can occur. The pain can become so strong that continuing to run almost becomes impossible. Serious pain is experienced during shocks as each foot strikes the ground. There is also high sensitivity to pressure on the inner part of the lowportion of the shinbone.

Possible causes
- Running on hard surface;
- Too abrupt transition from training on soft surface to training on hard surface;
- Shoes with insufficient shock absorption;
- Deviating position of the feet.

Possible solutions:
- Interrupting training;
- Running on soft surface;
- Gradual switching from training on soft surface to training on hard surface;
- Adapted running shoes with good shock absorption.

Photo & Illustration Credits

Cover Design: Jens Vogelsang
Inside Photos: Polar Electro Belgium
                   Pieter Desmedt-Jans
                   Octagon NV
Cover Photos: Bakke-Svensson WTC

IRONMAN

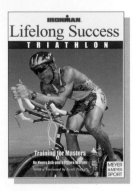

Ash/Warren
LIFELONG SUCCESS
Training for Masters

224 p., ISBN: 1-84126-103-3
$ 19.95 US / $ 29.95 CDN
£ 14.95 UK / € 18.90

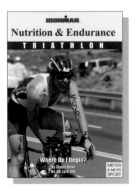

Sheila Dean
NUTRITION & ENDURANCE
Where Do I Begin?

144 p., ISBN: 1-84126-105-X
$ 17.95 US / $ 25.95 CDN
£ 12.95 UK / € 16.90

Ash/Warren
LIFELONG TRAINING
Advanced Training for Masters

272 p., ISBN: 1-84126-104-1
$ 19.95 US / $ 29.95 CDN
£ 14.95 UK / € 18.90

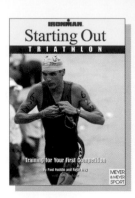

Huddle/Frey/Babbitt
STARTING OUT
**Training for Your First
Competition**

160 p., ISBN: 1-84126-101-7
$ 17.95 US / $ 25.95 CDN
£ 12.95 UK / € 16.90

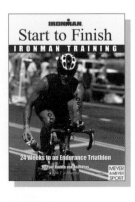

Huddle/Frey/Murphy
START TO FINISH
**24 Weeks to an Endurance
Triathlon**

178 p., ISBN: 1-84126-102-5
$ 17.95 US / $ 25.95 CDN
£ 12.95 UK / € 16.90

T. J. Murphy
THE UNBREAKABLE ATHLETE
Injury Prevention

152 p., ISBN: 1-84126-109-2
$ 17.95 US / $ 25.95 CDN
£ 12.95 UK / € 16.90

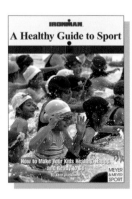

Kevin Mackinnon
A HEALTHY GUIDE TO SPORT
**How to Make Your Kids Healthy,
Happy, and Ready to Go**

128 p., ISBN: 1-84126-106-8
$ 17.95 US / $ 25.95 CDN
£ 12.95 UK / € 16.90

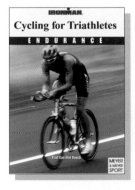

Paul Van Den Bosch
CYCLING FOR TRIATHLETES
Endurance

160 p., ISBN: 1-84126-107-6
$ 16.95 US / $ 24.95 CDN
£ 12.95 UK / € 16.95

**MEYER
& MEYER
SPORT**

MEYER & MEYER Sport • distribution@m-m-sports.com • www.m-m-sports.com

EDITION

OFFICIAL IRONMAN BOOKS ®

**Lisa Lynam
TRIATHLON FOR WOMEN**
A Mind-Body-Spirit Approach for Female Athletes

- This book aims to guide, educate and inspire women of any level how to get the most out of their triathlon endeavors, whether they are getting started with triathlons, moving on to develop as a smiling finisher at longer distance events, or emerging to a higher level of excellence in triathlon racing
- Includes aspects of fitness and skill development, smart nutrition choices, strength training, race planning, and mental aspects
- This uniquely written book aims to empower women in their own personal triathlon journeys to conquer the swim, bike, run with mind, body and spirit

About 200 pages, ISBN: 1-84126-108-4
$ 16.95 US / $ 24.95 CDN
£ 12.95 UK / € 16.95

**Kevin Mackinnon
TRIATHLON FOR YOUTH**
A Healthy Guide to Competition

- Triathlon is a fantastic endeavor for children because it promotes involvement in three "lifestyle" sports: swimming, biking, running
- This book will help young athletes from 12- to 16-years-old to begin a competitive career in triathlon, but in a healthy way that will enable them to develop to their full potential and make triathlon competition a part of their lifestyle
- This book will help parents and their teenagers develop a healthy training plan that will enhance many aspects of their lives
- The follow-up book to Kevin Mackinnon's "A Healthy Guide to Sport" for kids

About 160 p., ISBN: 1-84126-116-6
$ 16.95 US / $ 24.95 CDN
£ 12.95 UK / € 16.95

MEYER & MEYER Sport • distribution@m-m-sports.com • www.m-m-sports.com

MEYER &MEYER SPORT